A PENGUIN SPECIAL

Scargill and the Miners

Michael Crick was born in Northampton in 1958. He was educated at Manchester Grammar School and New College, Oxford, where he got a First in Philosophy, Politics and Economics. At Oxford he was heavily involved in both journalism and politics. He was President of the Union and Chairman of the Fabian Society, as well as Editor of *Cherwell* and Founder Editor of *The Oxford Handbook*. Since 1980 he has worked as a journalist with ITN in London. He has spent long periods abroad for ITN, notably in Poland for the rise of Solidarity in 1981, and covering the Israeli siege of Beirut in 1982. In 1982 he joined ITN's new Channel 4 News, where he is now a reporter, dealing mainly with politics and trade union affairs. During 1984 he covered the coal dispute extensively. His first book, *Militant*, was published in 1984.

Michael Crick

SCARGILL
and the Miners

Penguin Books

Penguin Books Ltd, Harmondsworth, Middlesex, England
Viking Penguin Inc., 40 West 23rd Street, New York, New York 10010, U.S.A.
Penguin Books Australia Ltd, Ringwood, Victoria, Australia
Penguin Books Canada Ltd, 2801 John Street, Markham, Ontario, Canada L3R 1B4
Penguin Books (N.Z.) Ltd, 182–190 Wairau Road, Auckland 10, New Zealand

First published 1985

Make and printed in Great Britain by
Richard Clay (The Chaucer Press) Ltd, Bungay, Suffolk
Filmset in 9/12pt Monophoto Photina by
Northumberland Press Ltd, Gateshead, Tyne and Wear

Contents

Acknowledgements

I would like to thank the following people for agreeing to be interviewed: Arthur Akeroyd, Don Baines, Trevor Bell, Arthur Brannigan, Owen Briscoe, Chris Butcher, Colin Clarke, Jack Collins, Bob Copping, Michael Eaton, Andrew Fearn, George Hayes, Jack Lally, John Liptrott, David Miller, Jimmy Miller, Austin Mitchell, Tony Morris, Jim Oldham, Roy Ottey, David Payne, Bert Ramelson, Jimmy Reid, Henry Richardson, Ron Rigby, Les Storey, Peter Tait, Jack Taylor, John Threlkeld, Sid Vincent, Howard Wadsworth, Jack Wake, Frank Watters and George Wilkinson. Some others who were interviewed did not wish to be named. Other people who I would have liked to speak to at length were understandably too busy because of the coal dispute.

The book could never have been written without friends and colleagues who have helped over the past ten weeks.

Above all, I am extremely grateful to my ITN colleague David Akerman. For ten weeks he was totally exploited. He researched, interviewed, advised, amended, arranged, encouraged, and even wrote some parts of the text. Without him the book could not have been written.

Andrew Curry of Channel 4 News went to great efforts to read the manuscript, and suggested numerous stylistic and factual changes.

Andrew Taylor of Huddersfield Polytechnic, author of *The Politics of the Yorkshire Miners* (Croom Helm, London, 1984) proposed a number of expert alterations and additions. I am grateful for his permission to draw upon much of his own work in this field.

Ian Ross, of ITN, advised and assisted, giving me the benefit of his long, unparalleled experience as an industrial correspondent. John Crick, Patricia Crick, Margaret Hounsell and Bill Hamilton read and suggested amendments to the text; Sandra Kiely and Alan Bellingham helped with the computer.

I must also thank the staff of the North Western and Yorkshire areas of the NUM, Barnsley Central Library, Manchester Central Library, the LSE Library, the British Newspaper Library, TV-am, Brook Productions, the *Sheffield Morning Telegraph*, and above all the staff of News Information at ITN, who were remarkably tolerant.

My editors, David Nicholas and Stewart Purvis, generously gave me permission to write the book, and sufficient time away from ITN to make it feasible.

I would have liked to have produced an index. Unfortunately, the speed with which the book was produced meant that this was not possible.

December 1984

A Note on the Structure of the National Union of Mineworkers

The organization of the National Union of Mineworkers operates on three levels – national, area and branch – and the NUM structure is broadly similar at each level.

The NUM is still very much a federal union comprising nineteen groups or 'areas', many of which are powerful trade unions in their own right. Fourteen of the areas are geographical: Cumberland, Derbyshire, Durham, Kent, Leicester, Midlands, Northumberland, North Wales, North Western, Nottingham, Scotland, South Derbyshire, South Wales and Yorkshire; and five areas are based on occupational divisions: Cokemen, Durham Mechanics, Scottish Enginemen, Colliery Officials and Staffs (COSA), and the Power Group.

The union has three elected national officials – the President, Vice-President and Secretary. The President and Secretary are officially equal in status, and are now elected in a ballot of the whole NUM membership for a period of five years (Arthur Scargill was elected before the rule was changed and is in office until he retires). The Vice-President, which in itself is not a full-time post, is elected by the Annual Conference every two years.

The National Executive Committee (NEC) is responsible for the day-to-day running of the union. It consists of the three elected national officials and currently twenty-three other members who represent the areas. Each area, no matter how small, is entitled to at least one member. The larger ones have more – Nottingham and South Wales have two members and Yorkshire three. The Executive members are chosen by the areas once every two years and will generally, but not always, be leading area full-time officials. The NUM President and Secretary cannot vote on the NEC, although the Vice-President can, and the President has a casting vote.

But the supreme governing body of the union is the Conference, which consists of delegates sent from each of the areas. Their numbers and voting strengths depend on the areas' relative membership figures. The Annual Conference meets in the first week of July, and Special Conferences can be called when the NEC wishes.

Each of the nineteen NUM areas is largely autonomous, with its own offices, rules, finances and staff. Each area has one or more elected full-time officials, and either the Area President or the General Secretary will be the more important depending on the area's tradition and personalities (for instance, the President is more important in Yorkshire and the General Secretary in Derbyshire). The larger areas also have full-time agents who deal with business in geographical parts of the area and groups of collieries.

Each area is governed by an Executive Committee and, in all the larger areas, also by an Area Council which consists of delegates from each of the area branches.

The branches to which individual members belong (called 'lodges' in Scotland and Wales) are based on collieries or other Coal Board workplaces, such as workshops. Each branch belongs to one of the NUM areas. The branch will have an elected committee and officials who include a Secretary, who deals with day-to-day business, a position which often turns out to be a full-time occupation, the Delegate, who represents the branch at NUM area and national level, and the President and Treasurer. The relative importance of each position varies from branch to branch and again depends on the personalities involved.

Introduction

They met, as usual, at the offices of the South Yorkshire NCB next door to Manvers Colliery. Normally, at such quarterly review meetings, the South Yorkshire NCB Director, George Hayes, and the area union officials went through the list of pits in the area alphabetically. Cortonwood comes fourth in that list. But that morning – Thursday 1 March 1984 – Hayes said he wanted to leave Cortonwood until last, because there were 'special problems' with it.

One by one the men discussed each of the other collieries, reviewing past performance and future prospects. Then came the special announcement: Cortonwood, with its 111 years of past performance, had five weeks of future prospects.

The NUM branch secretary at Cortonwood, Jack Wake, wasn't at the meeting. He was telephoned by Arnie Young, the South Yorkshire NUM agent, at about half past three that afternoon. 'It was a bombshell. I was completely taken aback. Arnie told me the pit was to close on 6 April – five weeks away.'[1]

George Hayes knew his announcement would be sensitive, but the Coal Board in London had asked him to take out 400,000 tonnes of production, and wanted him to do it by the end of the financial year. Cortonwood was losing £20 a tonne and was 'uneconomic'. But Hayes had 'no idea' that the 1 March meeting would have such far-reaching consequences.

Suez and the Falklands have been seen as the two most important events of post-war British history. Arguably, the 1984 coal dispute will come to be seen as a third.

On 6 March, five days after the Manvers meeting, the Coal Board had presented the leaders of the three mining unions with plans to reduce output in 1984 by four million tonnes (the NUM argued that the real figure was eight million), involving the closure of around twenty pits and the loss of about 20,000 jobs. Twelve days after the Cortonwood announcement, a majority of Britain's 180,000 miners were on strike. The leaders of Yorkshire, Scotland, Kent and South Wales one by one called their members out.

The 1984 strike will go down as the longest in the mining industry this century, and as one of the longest disputes ever experienced in any industry. It involved not just 150,000 miners and their families, but the transfer of thousands of police across the country and new, controversial, policing methods. It raised fundamental questions about the future of the unions, the Labour Party and the Government. For Margaret Thatcher and the Conservative administration Arthur Scargill became a second General Galtieri whom she was determined to defeat. In July 1984, Mrs Thatcher compared the miners with the Argentines in 1982, referring to them as 'the enemy within'.[2]

The strike would almost certainly never have happened twenty years ago, in the 1960s. In 1968, for instance, the Coal Board succeeded in closing fifty-five collieries and axing 55,000 jobs with hardly a protest. And these cuts were only a small part of the contraction of the coal industry that took place in those years. But at that time the level of unemployment was a tiny fraction of what it is today.

In the light of recent events it seems a remarkable fact that for nearly fifty years, between 1926 and 1972, there wasn't a single national strike in the mining industry – not even during the period of greatest contraction in the industry, from 1957 to 1971. And the miners weren't only losing their jobs in those years, but were also slipping behind in the pay league. In 1960 underground workers earned 10 per cent more than the average wage in manufacturing industry, but by 1971 this had dropped to 3 per cent below average.[3]

Throughout the period the miners' union Executive was politically dominated by the Right. Although the union did possess some well-known left-wing leaders, such as NUM Secretaries Arthur Horner and Will Paynter, who were both Communists, they found themselves 'prisoners' of their Executives, unable to lead the miners into the sort of action they themselves believed necessary.

In left-wing mythology the miners have a reputation as the 'shock troops' of the labour movement – the most militant section of the working class, able to inflict the most damaging blows upon the capitalist system. But in the post-war atmosphere of a nationalized industry, the miners' reputation began to look somewhat undeserved.

The NUM of the 1950s and 1960s seems far removed from the union of Arthur Scargill and Mick McGahey. Between 1957 and 1971 the union endured and tolerated pit closures and a contraction of the industry on a far greater scale than even Arthur Scargill's worst fears of what could happen under Ian MacGregor.

The politics of today's miners' union is in total contrast with the politics of its predecessors. The miners are now the most left wing of all the major unions; their leader, Arthur Scargill, is probably the most militant leader of a major union in living memory. The miners seem to have resumed their assigned role in the front line of the labour movement – though the movement itself seems unsure as to whether it wants them to play that role.

This book aims to put the 1984 coal dispute within the context of the remarkable transformation the NUM has undergone over the last fifteen years. In particular it focuses on the role of Arthur Scargill and the miners from Yorkshire, the NUM's largest area. How and why did that transformation come about, and how important was Scargill in that process? The book looks at the strikes of 1969, 1970, 1972 and 1974, and at aspects of the recent dispute, whose outcome is still unknown at the time of writing.

Much of the book has developed from my work as a producer and reporter with ITN's Channel 4 News. From the beginning of March 1984 I was working almost exclusively on the dispute, mostly out in the coalfields, talking to miners and their leaders. Throughout that period I was constantly trying to put the current events into a historical context and to look back at the events that led up to 1984. Parts of this book are therefore based on work I did at ITN.

Chapter 1

The Scot Who Went to Barnsley

When my term of office started, there were 583,000 people on the colliery books; when it ended, only 283,000 ... Without the understanding and cooperation of the unions and of the men themselves, this task could never have been accomplished.

– Lord Robens, Coal Board Chairman, 1961–71[1]

In October 1953 a 32-year-old Scot arrived in Barnsley to take up a new job. His name was Frank Watters. His new position was Communist Party organizer for the Yorkshire coalfield. A former miner from Lothian, Watters had gone down the pit at fourteen when he left school, and joined the Communist Party at eighteen, becoming active in union politics in Scotland. He had given up mining earlier in 1953 to become Communist organizer in the Scottish coalfield. After only eight months, the Communist Party had decided that Watters would be more useful in Yorkshire.

He had been reluctant to come to Barnsley at first. His mother had even appealed to the Party hierarchy not to make him go, but Watters knew it was his duty.

At that time the Communist Party, and the Left in general, were in a very weak position in the labour movement. The TUC and the Labour Party were firmly in the hands of the Right, largely because of the power of three unions who between them accounted for almost half the votes at the TUC and Labour Party conferences – the Transport and General Workers' Union, the General and Municipal Workers' Union, and the miners. Of the three, however, the miners seemed the most promising area for Communists and the Left to make progress. The miners had a historic reputation for militancy, and Communist Party members already held prominent positions in the union and were particularly strong in the Scottish and Welsh coalfields. The Communist Party therefore saw the Yorkshire coalfield as a vital target:

'The leadership wanted me to go to Yorkshire to help create a broad left wing to oppose the right wing in the area NUM,' recalls Watters. 'The members had shown by numerous unofficial strikes that they were militant, even if their leaders weren't. The leadership was not respected, so there was definitely potential there. The Party leadership believed that if the leaders of the Yorkshire NUM could be won over to the Left it would have a tremendous impact on the whole NUM, simply because Yorkshire is the biggest area. They wanted Yorkshire to join Scotland, South Wales and Kent, which would almost give a majority to the NUM Left. And because the NUM was one of the biggest unions at that time, they thought that if the NUM could be won over to the Left it would help transform the whole British labour movement. That's why I came to Barnsley in 1953.'[2]

Today, more than thirty years after the day he arrived in Barnsley, Watters looks back with some satisfaction. The plans set out by him and his superiors in 1953 have largely been realized, if not as quickly as they had hoped.

The Yorkshire miners now have a reputation as one of the most left wing groups of trade-unionists in Britain. The militancy of the Yorkshire NUM's 56,000 members – almost a third of the total membership of the NUM – has not only had a spreading influence throughout the British coalfields, but has also been used in the service of other groups of workers, notably at Grunwick in 1977 and on the nurses' picket lines in 1982. And, just as Watters had hoped, the radicalization of the Yorkshire miners in the late 1960s and early 1970s was the major cause of the subsequent swing from Right to Left in the NUM nationally. When Yorkshire's massive block vote moved to the Left it tipped the balance, though it wasn't until after Arthur Scargill became NUM President in 1982 that this transformation was complete.

Things have come a long way in the last thirty years. When a Communist member of the Yorkshire NUM Area Council put forward a motion in the late 1950s simply proposing support for the nurses in their demands for higher pay, he couldn't even find a seconder from more than a hundred other delegates.

The Yorkshire area was run by a right-wing autocracy throughout the 1940s, 1950s and 1960s. Yorkshire miners' leaders such as Joe Hall, Sid Schofield and Sam Bullough enjoyed good relations with the local Coal Board management. They would never dream of bringing Yorkshire's miners out on official strike. And they strongly supported the right-wing leadership of the Labour Party.

The situation in Yorkshire reflected the situation in the coal industry nationally. After the miners' defeat in the 1926 General Strike and lock-out and the earlier defeat they had suffered in 1921, leaders of what was then the Miners' Federation had concluded that in future the strike weapon should be used only as a last resort. It was to be almost fifty years before British miners held another national strike.

In the 1930s a more conciliatory, cooperative approach had developed between the miners and the coal owners. The long-awaited advent of nationalization of the mines, after the war, further reduced the traditional militancy of the British miners. When the NCB flags went up at each mine on 1 January 1947, after years of campaigning, the miners and their leaders believed the pits were finally 'theirs': they felt they had a duty not to disrupt things. Indeed, in the years following nationalization, many of the men who held leading positions in the new Coal Board had been miners. Perhaps the best example of this was Jim Bowman (later knighted), a former NUM Vice-President, who was Chairman of the Coal Board from 1956 to 1961. Many people feel that until the early 1970s NUM leaders did not always get all they could for their members – a view held even by many on the Right, including Joe Gormley. and by some leading members of the Coal Board.

The National Union of Mineworkers was not always blessed with outstanding leaders. The Presidency of the NUM – officially equal in status to the Secretaryship – was at times held by weak characters, in some cases because no one of any calibre could be persuaded to do the job. One of the most outstanding NUM figures, Sam Watson, the right-wing leader of the Durham miners for nearly thirty years, preferred to remain a leader in his own area, rather than go for a national position. In contrast, on the Left, two Communist NUM Secretaries, Arther Horner and Will Paynter, found themselves powerless amid a right-wing Executive. Will Lawther, for example, NUM President from 1939 to 1954, used to boast that he never had to spend his union salary. and managed to live on union expenses. He was not the last to do so.

Although the Miners' Federation of Great Britain had become the National Union of Mineworkers in 1945. it still remained very much a federal organization – much more so than any other trade union. The National Executive was little more than a collection of local miners' leaders, many of whom, in their own areas, were powerful trade union figures. The federal nature of the union, though, gave even the smallest constituent groups a place on the Executive, and this always acted against the Left. They could traditionally count on two of the largest areas, Scotland and South Wales – whose representatives were often Communists – as well as the much smaller Kent coalfield, and sometimes Derbyshire. Scotland had the Moffat brothers, Abe and Alex, while Wales produced both Arthur Horner and Will Paynter. All the other areas, though, could almost always be counted on to vote with the Right, including several tiny non-geographical craftsmen's groups who all had men on the Executive in spite of their relatively small size. This meant that the Left were badly outnumbered – by two or three to one.

The union's constitution also provided a major obstacle to militancy. At the Re-organization Conference in August 1944, right-wing areas looked back to 1926, when divisions between areas had contributed to the miners' defeat. So it was agreed that in future a national strike would be called only if there was overwhelming support for it. The result was NUM Rule 43 (see Appendix), which, until 1971, required a two-thirds majority in favour of strike action before a national strike could go ahead. (In fact, such a ballot was held for the first time only in 1970.)

Andrew Taylor, author of *The Politics of the Yorkshire Miners*, points out: 'During the 1940s and 1950s the miners formed the core of the right-wing official support for the policies of the Labour Party leadership, first under Attlee and subsequently under Gaitskell.' At Labour Party conferences the Right depended heavily on the NUM President, Will Lawther, and Sam Watson of Durham, to deliver the miners' votes. The Yorkshire area was typical of the national picture and also took a Gaitskellite position. In 1953, amid all the bitterness between Hugh Gaitskell and Nye Bevan, the branch at Thorne Colliery near Doncaster was attacked by the area leadership for holding a meeting with Bevan as guest speaker. Later the area supported Gaitskell on nuclear weapons. And when it came to sponsoring MPs, the Yorkshire NUM could be relied on to return to Parliament men who would be loyal to the Party leadership.

Yet that was not the whole picture, either nationally or in Yorkshire, as Watters knew when he arrived in Barnsley in 1953. For, while the NUM had right-wing leaders, the miners themselves were one of the most strike-prone groups of British workers. While there was never any question of an official national strike, mining still managed to have the worst disputes record of any industry. In 1956, for instance, the official figures show that mining accounted for 78·4 per cent of all British strikes. Over the years from 1947 to 1963 mining accounted for about two thirds of all strikes and about 30 per cent of working days lost.[4] But the official statistics exaggerate the true picture a little, simply because the Coal Board was much better than other industries at keeping strike records. Nevertheless, throughout the twenty years following nationalization, the coal industry suffered hundreds of small strikes in individual collieries or groups of collieries. And almost invariably these disputes were unofficial, without the backing of the area or national NUM leadership.

The Yorkshire coalfield was particularly afflicted by strikes. The Ministry of Labour noted in 1965: 'In coal mining, Yorkshire has accounted for 46 per cent of all days lost in the industry during 1950–64, though the proportion of mining employees in that region averaged only 20 per cent, over these years.'[5] In the words of one commentator, 'the Yorkshire coalfield has been an important percentage of an important percentage'.[6]

Why the Yorkshire coalfield should have been so much more susceptible to strikes than the other coalfields is unclear. One reason must have been the piece-work system, whereby, instead of being paid a basic wage, miners were paid according to the tonnage mined, and then also received a large number of variable allowances to take account of breakdowns, water, faults in the seam and height. This system, which was particularly complex in parts of Yorkshire, led to constant arguments over pay, and to unofficial strikes.

It was a remarkable paradox. During the 1950s and 1960s one of the most actively militant groups of workers in Britain was led and represented by a very non-militant and right-wing leadership. Left-wingers within the Yorkshire Area NUM were in a minority amongst the union's officials and often isolated. Indeed, at times they were positively suppressed.

But the Left could count on strong support at many Yorkshire pits. At some collieries the branch secretary, regarded as the most important official, because he dealt directly with the pit manager, was often on the Left. And the unofficial strikes were frequently led by these branch officials. But the more politically important officer in union terms, the branch delegate, who had to deal directly with the area leadership of the NUM, was often on the Right. This meant that the Yorkshire NUM Area Council, comprising delegates from each pit, and the Area Executive, were strongly right wing. And in many other collieries the Right were in total control. Many of these local NUM officials developed a close, cosy relationship with management and an understanding that ensured there was little industrial trouble at their pits.

For a few men the post of branch secretary in a Yorkshire pit proved to be highly lucrative. Some were effectively being paid twice. Because secretaries spent so much time on union business and very little, or even none, actually working as miners, it was traditional for the official's wages to be paid by the NUM: perhaps two or three shifts a week by the local branch and two or three by the Yorkshire area headquarters in Barnsley. But, in many cases, branch secretaries were also paid by the colliery, as if they were completing their full quota of shifts. This meant that some branch secretaries could be earning up to ten shifts a week. One or two ended up as quite wealthy men.

Through the network of branch officials the right-wing Yorkshire area leadership succeeded in keeping a firm grip on its union. Some local officials had ambitions to become MPs and knew that it was the leadership of the Yorkshire area which decided who should receive NUM sponsorship for Parliamentary nominations. So long as branch officials were loyal to the area leadership, the leadership was prepared to turn a blind eye to wayward practices which might be going on locally.

The Left, however, benefited by the informal separation of the Yorkshire NUM into four smaller geographical divisions called 'panels' – North Yorkshire, Barnsley, Doncaster and South Yorkshire. The panels are unofficial NUM groupings which correspond to the official Coal Board divisions. Each panel has its own full-time agent and elected officials, and meets monthly to discuss Area Council and Executive business. Even though panels have no constitutional powers, at times in the past they acted as an alternative left-wing power base against the area leadership.

For several years the Doncaster panel had been the most militant, and had been involved in many of the major unofficial strikes. In contrast, the bedrock of the Yorkshire NUM Right was the North Yorkshire panel. The leadership could always count on the North Yorkshire pits around Leeds, Pontefract and Wakefield to back them. And because this panel was better organized than the other three many of the Yorkshire area officials at this time came from North Yorkshire.

In his early years in Yorkshire, Frank Watters took a keen interest in the unofficial strike activity for which the coalfield was renowned. His work among miners was largely confined to Communist Party members, as might be expected. Watters arranged regular Communist NUM caucus meetings at which Party members would plan their strategy for the area. They drew up resolutions to be put to local branches and to the Area

Council. Watters and the caucus would decide who should stand for election for each position in the area. He says the Communist Party at that stage made a deliberate decision to concentrate its efforts on changing the composition of the Yorkshire NUM Area Council, which was the area's top decision-making body: 'we concentrated upon getting our best cadres as delegates to the Council. This was always difficult because the delegate was usually a part-time trade unionist, while branch secretaries were usually full-time.'[7]

The two effective leaders of the Left in Yorkshire, Jock Kane and Sammy Taylor, were both Communists. They were leaders who could arouse an audience and win respect and support among men who might not necessarily agree with their politics. Kane was a Scot who worked at Hatfield Main, in the Doncaster panel, while Taylor, the Chairman of the Yorkshire area Communist Party, came from Barnsley. Both men stood for a whole succession of positions in the Yorkshire area, almost always unsuccessfully. Frank Watters would run the election campaigns.

But in time both Kane and Taylor were elected to important positions within the area. As early as 1959, Sammy Taylor secured a place as the Yorkshire area's rank-and-file member on the NUM National Executive, and he became Yorkshire Compensation Agent in 1964. In 1966, Jock Kane was elected Area Financial Secretary, and later joined Taylor on the National Executive. Having these men in such key positions in the union enabled the Left to know what was going on, and to see all the relevant documents.

Even though he was the Communist Party organizer, Watters knew that the Left would only make progress if there was a broad alliance between Communists and left-wing Labour Party members in the Yorkshire NUM. But in the late 1950s there were very few Labour left-wingers, and any coordination between themselves was generally confined to informal gatherings in the pub after Area Council meetings or telephone contact. Cooperation between the Communists and the Labour Left was difficult because of this, and because of the distrust and suspicion felt by people on both sides. Watters often found himself arguing against members of his own party who did not want to work with outsiders.

In about 1960, though, Communist and Labour left-wingers began to meet together on a regular, more formal basis, just as Watters had planned. After Sammy Taylor's election to the NUM Executive in 1959 the Left had achieved another success in 1960, when the Yorkshire area nominated the Scottish Communist Alex Moffat for the NUM Presidency. Soon left-wing miners from the Barnsley panel started meeting for discussions in a room in the Queen's Hotel, opposite Barnsley railway station.

Later, others, mainly from the Doncaster panel, began holding meetings in the Danum Hotel in the centre of Doncaster, one of the town's best hotels. Among them were Jock Kane and Sammy Taylor, Tommy Mullany from Hatfield Main and Owen Briscoe from Markham Main. Soon the meetings in the Danum got bigger, and began to involve miners from Barnsley as well.

In about 1964 or 1965 the group constituted itself on a formal basis. The meetings occurred more regularly in various pubs and clubs in Barnsley and Doncaster. Among other miners who started attending were Ron Rigby, NUM secretary at Shafton Workshops; Don Baines, NUM delegate from Brierley Colliery; Jim Oldham, NUM secretary at Hickleton Main in the Doncaster panel; George Wilkinson from Houghton Main; and two Communists from Wharncliffe-Woodmoor, Tom Degnan and Peter Tait.

This group was in turn joined by other miners: Mick Welsh from Brodsworth; Martin Redmond from Doncaster; Jimmy Miller, a Scottish Communist from Kellingley Colliery in North Yorkshire; Ian Ferguson, a Scot from Yorkshire Main; and a young former Communist, Arthur Scargill, who had just been elected branch delegate at Woolley. According to most accounts, though, Scargill was not one of the original members of the group.

After a while the regular meeting place for this new Left group became the Albert Club in Cudworth, a village three miles north-east of Barnsley. A room in the club would be booked by Ron Rigby, who got it cheaply through an arrangement he had to hold his NUM branch meetings there. Generally the group met once a month, after National Executive meetings on a Monday or Friday evening; the meetings started at seven o'clock in the evening, and lasted two or three hours. Mick Welsh might sit in the chair and draw up an informal agenda. Sometimes Jock Kane acted as chairman.

'The main thing was to get people elected to vacancies in the area and nationally where they could exert influence,' says Don Baines. 'Policies were secondary at that stage. The main task was to identify vacancies and identify candidates for them.'[8]

The group never really adopted a formal title, but was sometimes referred to by members as 'the Left', the 'Yorkshire Left' or the 'Yorkshire

Miners' Forum'. (From now on I shall refer to it as the 'Yorkshire Left'.)
Membership was very restricted. George Wilkinson remembers: 'You had
to be committed Left to get in. We had to vet new members, and one or
two were rejected because we weren't sure about them.'[9] Almost like a
secret society, the person who recommended a new member was virtually
held responsible for him measuring up to standard. Sometimes new
members would be brought in for a specific tactical purpose. For instance,
the present Yorkshire NUM President, Jack Taylor, then only on the
branch committee at Manvers Main, was invited to join the Yorkshire Left
because they were looking for new blood in South Yorkshire to challenge
leading right-wingers such as Jack Layden, the Maltby delegate.

Even today, some of those involved in the Left are reluctant to talk about
their former activities, and it is only recently that any details of their work
have been made public.[10] When it began, the Yorkshire Left had to meet
amid great secrecy and intrigue, because the area leadership would have
cracked down on them. Constitutionally, such caucuses within the NUM
are illegal, even though right-wingers had been holding the same kind of
meetings for years.

Frank Watters generally kept away from the meetings, not wishing to
offend those who might be hostile to his presence as a Communist Party
organizer. But naturally he kept in close touch with what was going on.

Within the group, relations between those who were Communists and
the rest were sometimes uneasy. One member recalls: 'There were arguments that some people were coming along to the meetings having been
mandated, especially later on when the group got bigger. There were
disputes about whether there had been separate meetings beforehand.'
Another says: 'It was often felt that members of the Communist Party had
received their marching orders in advance.' Peter Tait admits that indeed
the Communists did sometimes caucus beforehand.

There was also some rivalry between men from the Barnsley panel
and the Doncaster panel, the latter considering itself to be more 'pure' in
its socialism.

The Yorkshire Left would formulate resolutions and then agree on
which members should try to get them passed by their branches. Often the
motions would be lost at branch level, but for the Left it was still important
to get their views aired at the pit. On some occasions the resolutions were
passed. The Left also decided what attitude to take on other motions
coming up at Area Council.

When, occasionally, stories about the Yorkshire Left meetings leaked out, members said the group was simply a discussion group to talk about 'compensation cases'. On one occasion the Area Executive hauled about eight members of the group before it in the Area Council Chamber and accused them of acting unconstitutionally. 'You've got to stop these meetings,' the Yorkshire President, Sam Bullough, insisted. 'All go into the Executive Room and make your minds up what you're going to do about it.' They had to sign an undertaking that no more caucuses would be held in future. It made no difference.

There are several reasons why the Yorkshire Left should have suddenly emerged at this time when the Left in Yorkshire had been so weak before.

The new miners' day-release courses at Leeds and Sheffield universities, started in the 1950s, were one important influence. Most members of the group had been on or would attend such courses, which were organized and financed jointly by the NUM and the Coal Board. The student miners were taught economics, politics and industrial law, and learnt how to express themselves both on paper and orally. At Leeds the mining students took part in debates, and then listened to tapes of their speeches. Many of the teachers were strongly left wing – among them Michael Barratt Brown, Royden Harrison, John Hughes and Jim MacFarlane at Sheffield University, and, at Leeds, E. P. Thompson. The day-release courses educated miners who had frequently left school at fourteen or fifteen, and did a great deal to raise their political awareness. The present Yorkshire President, Jack Taylor, who attended a course at Sheffield, says they enabled miners to meet and talk with men from other parts of the coalfield. Inevitably they swapped ideas, and the students became friends. Large numbers of the students went on to be very active in the NUM, if they weren't already active before they went on the course. Today, a majority of the Yorkshire full-time officials and the Area Council delegates have attended such schemes.

A second factor was the immigration into Yorkshire of miners from other more militant coalfields. Several members of the group were Scots. Jock Kane had walked down from Scotland in 1926 when he found that no Scottish pit would employ him after his activities in the 1926 lock-out. Jim Oldham had come from County Durham the following year, with his family. His father had been on the union committee at a colliery which had stayed out long after other miners had gone back. The coal owner had wanted to lower wages even more than elsewhere, and the Oldham family, too, were banned from working in the area: 'We were evicted from our miner's cottage, so I grew up with a chip on my shoulder. I didn't trust the employers. They made me a militant.'[11] Jimmy Miller was a much later immigrant, coming down from Fife in 1964 when his home pit closed. Peter Tait was also a Scot.

Gradually the Yorkshire Left grew in size and influence. Members of the group succeeded in getting themselves elected to the Yorkshire Area Council and to the Executive. And other left-wingers who got elected at various branches were gradually brought into the Left group.

Frank Watters had been active in the coalfield throughout this time. In 1967 the Communist Party decided that the miners were no longer so important, since the NUM had become such a relatively small union because of the contraction of the coal industry. The Party asked Watters to go to Birmingham to become District Secretary and work on the new militancy among the car workers of the West Midlands. His period in Yorkshire had been a long, difficult time, and the Party moved him away just as his work in the area began to bear fruit: 'The fourteen years transformed the coalfield and created the conditions for people like Arthur Scargill to reap the harvest. Without those fourteen years, Scargill couldn't have emerged.'[12]

After his departure, Watters maintained the friendships and contacts he had built in Yorkshire. Today he is back living in Barnsley. where officially he works for the *Morning Star*, but often he can be found in the Yorkshire miners' offices. He still sees Arthur Scargill regularly, and acted as his 'agent' when Scargill stood for NUM office.

This is not the last we shall see of him in this story.

Chapter 2

The Boy Who Would Be King

At the age of fifteen I decided that the world was wrong and I wanted to put it right, virtually overnight if possible.

– Arthur Scargill[1]

Inside the hall, the miners of Woolley Colliery, near Barnsley, were gathering for their monthly union meeting. Behind the table at the front sat the right-wing 'old guard', men who had served as NUM branch officials at Woolley for years. Outside, an eighteen-year-old apprentice was arguing with the men on the door who seemed determined not to let him in. At last, that night, the young man gave up arguing, and went home in anger, determined that he would get his way – eventually.

A few weeks earlier the young man had caused uproar at the previous branch meeting, when he had stood up to address his fellow union members for the first time in his life. His speech, on the subject of training for mining apprentices, had been regarded as so outrageous by the men at the table that they had all stood up and walked out.

The year was 1956. That angry young man was Arthur Scargill. He believes the incidents he had been involved in were typical of the way in which the Yorkshire NUM was run at that time: 'I suffered terribly as a result of the right-wing domination ... The leadership were responsible for some of the worst things that could be done to any workman, let alone a trade-unionist ... the right wing at that time had guards on the door of the branch meeting and wouldn't allow me to enter the room ... here was a young man of eighteen years of age, being denied the right, *physically*, even to go to his own branch meeting. This was the sort of experience I have in the trade-union movement.'[2]

Few miners can have suffered more political victimization than Scargill when he was in his teens. At one point things got so bad that he thought of giving it all up and joining the fire service. Perhaps he should have followed his initial inclination on leaving school, and that of his parents: like most mining families the Scargills hadn't wanted their son to become a miner – Arthur's mother, in particular, was 'passionately' against it.

When he had left school at fifteen he had in fact applied for jobs in local engineering factories. 'I thought I was the greatest gift to engineering since the invention of the wheel. Somehow no one seemed to agree . . . So I went into the colliery.'[3] It may have been that there were few vacancies for unqualified school-leavers in the Barnsley engineering industry at that time, or simply that he didn't make a good impression. Either way, the current right-wing leaders of the engineering union, Gavin Laird and Terry Duffy, ought to be grateful.

Arthur Scargill was born on 11 January 1938, the first and only child of Harold and Alice Scargill. His mother was thirty-two when he was born. She had previously lost a child and had been told that she would be unable to have any more. So Arthur's arrival was quite a surprise.

The Scargill family lived on a hillside overlooking a valley, in Worsbrough Dale, a small, quite attractive village, just south of Barnsley. Apart from short stays in London during his NUM Presidency, Scargill has never lived anywhere other than Worsbrough. His first home, 27 Pantry Hill, was a one-up, one-down mining cottage with no gas or electricity, and only a storm lamp for lighting. There was no inside lavatory, or hot water – just cold water from a tap at the kitchen sink. Neither the house nor the street exists any longer. The family moved to a more comfortable council house with two bedrooms and a bathroom when he was three.

Scargill remembers: 'Worsbrough was a very close-knit mining community; it seemed to me everyone in the world lived there. I've seen men boxing, Sunday afternoons, bare knuckled, for a side stake of 2s 6d; I've seen whippet racing, pigeon racing. It was a complete community. Nowhere was there such a growth of brass bands and marvellous choirs as Yorkshire: the Welsh haven't got a monopoly. And when we had a disaster – 12 or 15 men killed in a pit – the sense of grief and shock was something I've not witnessed anywhere else. As a child I had that sense of a mining community setting themselves apart – not because they wanted to but because they were compelled to.'[4]

One of Arthur's first memories, as a tiny child, is of going out with the dog to meet his father – who every day walked five miles home from the pit. His father's approach was hidden by the brow of a hill, and the first sign of him was the sound of clogs on the cobblestones, at which point the dog went mad barking. Arthur's childhood was hard but not impoverished: 'We never had any luxuries in life. My father was always suffering from some sort of infirmity. so he didn't work as much as a normal miner.'⁵

The Second World War broke out when Arthur was only twenty months old. His father went into the Royal Air Force and served in West Africa, while Alice Scargill worked in a munitions factory for the duration of the hostilities. Arthur remembers the war having a 'damaging effect on our family life. My mother was having to work and I was an only child being left with my grandparents.'⁶

He was educated at the village junior school in Worsbrough. One teacher later remembered: 'He was always saying "I've done, miss – what shall I do next?" When I was on yard duty, he'd pop up in front of me, asking questions. He liked puzzling you, and arguing for the sake of arguing – but he kept you on your toes.'⁷ There is also some evidence that Scargill was badly bullied at school.

But when it came to leaving primary school Scargill refused to take the 11-plus, because if he had passed it would have meant going to the grammar school in Barnsley, and he didn't want to leave Worsbrough. 'In retrospect I can see that I was wrong.' Instead he went to White Cross Secondary School, which is now Worsbrough High School. There he was put in the B stream, 'because I refused to try'.⁸

But Scargill received a good education at home. He remembers that his house was full of books: 'the Bible, Shakespeare, we had everything'.⁹ From an early age Arthur read avidly – often at the rate of a book a day. In particular, when he was about thirteen he read Jack London's *The Iron Heel* and Robert Tressell's *The Ragged Trousered Philanthropists*, which he later said 'were the books that formed my political opinions'.¹⁰ He has said that Jack London was 'more responsible for me being a socialist than any-thing'.¹¹ He also read about starvation in Africa and about how the Americans and Canadians were producing so much wheat they had to burn it in railway engines.

Both Scargill's parents, in their separate ways, seem to have had a tremendous influence upon him. Arthur's father was active in the NUM, but never held office in the union, or any other political position:

'I owe more to my father than anybody else for my introduction into the trade union movement,' says Scargill. 'And even today if I have a problem I think it's a very good thing to discuss it with my father because I get a lot of common sense from him – a really detached view of the situation; and invariably it's the right sort of decision he produces.'¹²

Today, Harold Scargill lives with his son and his family in Worsbrough. He's nearly eighty and has been a member of the Communist Party all his life – and a fairly hard-line one at that. 'He takes the Russian line on Poland,' according to his son.[13]

Harold Scargill took his son to political meetings from an early age. But Arthur has said that although his father was a great political influence upon him he never forced him to be involved in politics. 'He left me to make my own judgments. Obviously the fact that the *Daily Worker* came into my house . . . *Reynolds News* . . . *Tribune* and other left-wing papers and books was bound to have an effect.'[14]

His mother was 'strictly non-political'. 'We had a warm, lovely relationship,' he says of her.[15] She doted on Arthur: 'She was a very religious woman . . . she had a brother crippled for life and a father who died at forty-four from working in the pit. But all she wanted was for me to have a safe job.'[16]

His mother died in 1956, when Arthur was eighteen. 'It really hammered me. I was as close to her as anyone can be to their parents. I didn't eat a slice of bought bread till she died – she always baked it. Every time I've achieved something I've felt sad she wasn't there to see it.'[17]

Instead of going to a local pit at fifteen, he signed on at Woolley Colliery, a large pit several miles away, on the north side of Barnsley, near Wakefield (it now lies just on the eastern side of the M1 near to Woolley Edge service station). Arthur had calculated that the shift at Woolley was half an hour shorter than elsewhere. He remembers the first day there so well that his account of it has become a set performance.

'I left home at four in the morning with a bottle of water and some bread and jam for snap, and travelled on two buses to get there.

'I had to wait in this engineer's office, where they had the biggest clock outside Big Ben.

'He eventually arrived and, looking at us through his thick glasses, said "Oh, you're t'new lot are you."

'He took us underground – I thought we were going down into Hell – and we came to a place where there were five great steel belts making the most awful noise.'[18]

The new recruits were in the screening sheds where men had to pick muck and stone from the coal.

'You couldn't see more than two yards for dust, and the noise was so intense you had to speak with your hands. I had to scrape the caked dust from my lips before I could eat my sandwiches. I couldn't understand how such awful working conditions could exist in 1953.'[19]

'The foreman, a chap with one eye, was called Melson, and there were two sets of people in the section: us – and the disabled rejects of society.

'I saw men with one arm and one leg, men crippled and mentally retarded. I nearly turned and ran. I thought "I can't work in this lot," but I did for a year and I suppose it had a direct effect on my life.

'I saw people who should never have been working, having to work to live. They were a danger to themselves and everyone else.'[20]

Scargill spent two and a half years in the screening plant before going underground to become a pony driver. Today he likes to remind people that his pony was called 'King'.

In 1955 Scargill tried to join the Labour Party: 'I thought that the political party of the day, as far as the working class was concerned, was the Labour Party. All the kids around this area, their fathers supported the Labour Party and I thought well it's a natural thing to do, we're all Labour in this village. I wrote to the Labour Party and I said: "Is there any such organisation as a Labour Youth Party, and if so, could you give me some details, and could I possibly join?" Nobody ever replied.'[21]

In Barnsley at that time the Labour Party was a weak, run-down organization, controlled by the Right. Not prepared to give up straight away, Scargill wrote to the *Daily Herald* to see if they could help him join. Again there was no reply. Finally, and very angry with the Labour Party, he sent a letter to the Communist newspaper, the *Daily Worker*. Within twenty-four hours a Communist Party organizer was round at his house with an application form. The Barnsley Young Communist League (YCL) minutes for 31 March 1955 record: 'Today the comrades visited Billy Smart's circus. Arthur Scargill and Derek Stubbings joined the party. The membership is now 11.'[22]

It was clearly a momentous occasion for the Young Communist League. A photo of Scargill and Stubbings appeared in *Challenge*, the YCL newspaper. 'Arthur Scargill and Derek Stubbings are old schoolmates and say they do everything together,' the journal proclaimed.[23]

Within a few months Scargill had become Barnsley YCL secretary and was making a big impact on the branch. That autumn he was on a YCL delegation which went to see Barnsley's MP, Roy Mason, about shortening National Service 'call-up time'. By October 1955 *Challenge* was quoting

Scargill as saying that the Barnsley branch had increased its membership to twenty-five.

Scargill has often claimed in recent years that under his leadership membership of the Barnsley YCL rose rapidly to several hundred (600 was the figure he gave in one interview). Frank Watters feels that Scargill has rather exaggerated these figures.

Watters had met Scargill's father soon after he arrived in Barnsley in October 1953. Only months after Scargill had joined the YCL Watters had realized that Arthur had tremendous potential. One of his earliest memories of Scargill is of him speaking from the same platform as the Communist Party General Secretary, Harry Pollitt, at a public meeting in Barnsley.

The youth sections of both the Labour Party and the Communist Party at that time were much less intense and more enjoyable organizations to belong to. The YCL wasn't just politics. As Secretary of his YCL Scargill organized a whole range of political and non-political activities – political talks, debates, jazz concerts and trips to the seaside.

One former member of the Barnsley YCL recalls: 'He was never shy of voicing his opinions even then. Every Sunday afternoon we had meetings, Marxist classes, poetry readings, rambles. He was very fond of Burns, I remember.

'In the Marxist classes he was always very dynamic, always asking questions and wanting to get people in to talk to us who knew more about the subject than what we did.'[24]

Within eighteen months of joining the YCL, Scargill had been elected to its National Committee at the 1956 Congress. His progress may have been aided by the fact that the Congress also presented Scargill with the Gallacher Cup on behalf of Yorkshire, for managing to increase sales of *Challenge* from seventy to 150 in just five months.

On the National Committee Scargill took an interest in industrial work. But during his four years on the Committee he never proceeded to higher office, and did not stand out from the other committee members. It is interesting to note that another leading YCL member at that time was Jimmy Reid, from Clydeside, who later became YCL Secretary. He and Scargill became quite close friends. Both men achieved national prominence at more or less the same time – in the early 1970s (Reid in the Upper Clyde Shipbuilders work-in) – and in similar circumstances. They remained friends until the 1984 dispute, when Reid was publicly very critical of Scargill's decision not to hold a ballot.

Scargill also became Chairman of the Yorkshire District YCL, and when the Campaign for Nuclear Disarmament was formed got involved in its activities, and became Chairman of the CND Yorkshire area.

It was only some time after joining the Young Communists that Scargill began to take an interest in union affairs, since, he says, he had begun to feel that real power lay with the working class. At Woolley he started complaining to the pit management – about leaving times and about ice in the pit. But Scargill soon found opposition – from other miners: 'the older miners viewed me with great suspicion because it was unknown for a young miner to be involved in trade unionism'.[25]

So, when he addressed his first union meeting, he found no sympathy: 'It was a fantastic situation. I stood on my feet, and I thought I was speaking reasonably eloquently to this meeting, but it was in a political sense, and the miners in the meeting, led by the right wing of the branch at that time, simply just stood up and walked out of the meeting. I was shattered.'[26]

Over the next few years Scargill found he was fighting the right-wing leadership of his union just as much as the pit bosses: 'the union leaders were well to the right of Genghis Khan. I don't know if they were corrupt, but they were bosom pals with management.'[27]

The branch leadership at Woolley was so right wing and anti-Communist that even the area leadership thought they had gone too far at times. In choosing Woolley because it had a shorter shift, Scargill had accidentally ended up at one of the most right-wing pits in Yorkshire, and this must have greatly affected his political outlook.

Scargill was badly victimized by the officials of his own NUM branch for being a Communist. He believes that it was they who arranged for the colliery management to put him on an awkward shift. It meant him starting at six in the evening and not getting home until four or five in the morning, because there was no public transport. It was a fairly miserable period for Scargill at work: 'The idea was a very simple one – to get rid of me, to force me into a position where I would no longer tolerate the intolerable shifts and get out of the industry. Well, I was equally determined that they wouldn't get rid of me.'[28]

Scargill was fierce in defending the rights of his fellow young miners. He demanded an NUM youth conference and argued for the right for young people to be fully involved in union affairs. At one point Scargill led a strike among young miners at the pit over training, and his branch responded by expelling him from the union. He had to be reinstated by the Yorkshire NUM Area President.

In 1957 Scargill was elected by the men at Woolley to go to the World Youth Festival in Moscow. By now Scargill's Communist views were known throughout the colliery, and the men obviously thought he would be an appropriate choice to send to the Soviet Union. 'Some of the lads at my pit seem to think that I won't get back,' he wrote in the YCL newspaper before his visit.[29] As part of a 1,650-strong delegation from Britain, he met Khrushchev and Bulganin at a reception in the Kremlin, and he says he openly attacked members of the Soviet leadership for the denigration of Stalin which had begun only the year before: 'I told them, "You can't get rid of him by removing his body from the mausoleum, you know. You can't rewrite history and he did play a valuable part during World War Two."'[30]

In May 1960, at the age of only twenty-two, Scargill stood as a Communist candidate for the North Ward of Worsbrough Urban District Council. He pledged to 'fight for the needs of the people both young and old, to make Worsbrough a model mining village with all the social amenities for all the people', and he called for 'a Socialist system of society in which the Communist party will play a major role'.[31]

There were only two candidates, both of them socialist. Scargill got 138 votes and his Labour opponent, Alderman Charles Boland, 945. It was the first and last time Scargill stood in a public election.

May 1960 was a busy month for Scargill. Only a few days before the local election he had been a leader of an unofficial strike at Woolley, not against the pit management, but against his own union branch officials. A large number of the men at Woolley – mostly younger members – wanted NUM branch meetings to be held on Sunday evenings instead of Friday evenings. Many of them worked on Fridays and they said they lost a day's wages and a week's bonus by going to the Friday meeting. Scargill believed the branch officials were deliberately trying to deter left-wingers from attending. In turn, one official said the dispute was 'Communist inspired' and called for Communists to be expelled from the union. It was only resolved when Scargill and a thousand supporters marched through Barnsley and a delegation went to the area headquarters to get the support of the Yorkshire area leadership for Sunday meetings. According to Scargill: 'The net effect was a transformation from an attendance of forty to an attendance of about 200 per time, and this had a profound effect upon the branch and, of course, increased my scope and standing and influence in the pit as a whole.'[32]

Shortly afterwards, Scargill was elected to the branch committee for the first time.

Scargill met his future wife, Anne, in the same year. Arthur had called to deliver a message at the home of a member of the Wooley branch committee, Elliott Harper. The door was answered by the official's eighteen-year-old daughter, Anne. They got chatting. She told him she wanted to learn to drive. Arthur offered to teach her. Their first date was a Young Communist League debate. 'We knew in a week that we wanted to get married.'[33] On 16 September 1961, they were married in Gawber Parish Church. A year later they had a daughter, Margaret, their only child.

Scargill was also selected to attend a part-time day-release course for miners at Leeds University, studying Social History and Industrial Relations. For three years he spent one day a week at Leeds, and says it was one of the determining influences in his life: 'It taught me to think and to question. I began to dissect everything that came my way in minute detail, so that I could argue.'[34]

In late 1962 or 1963 (there is no record of exactly when), Scargill left the Young Communist League. The circumstances of the departure are still not certain and Scargill has given varying accounts of them to different journalists. This is not to suggest that Scargill is trying to hide anything – he may not remember the exact details and there were probably several different reasons for his decision.

Scargill told Chapman Pincher of the Daily Express, in 1977, that he had been 'expelled': 'because I wouldn't stick to any rigid party line'.[35] The 'expulsion' story was also told to Ann Leslie of the Daily Mail, in December that year. But on other occasions Scargill has said that he simply resigned.

Perhaps the fullest explanation of his departure was given to John Mortimer: 'I disagreed with the Russians not allowing dissidents to leave the country ... I also objected to the moving of Stalin's body outside the mausoleum and changing the name of Stalingrad. It would be like us trying to pretend Churchill never existed. It was distorting history. And I didn't like the personal discipline of the party. They wanted me to sell the Daily Worker on Fridays, but I had union business to look after on a Friday so I joined the Co-operative Party.'[36]

On television in 1975, however, Scargill took a less Stalinist line, saying he disagreed with the Soviet Union's censorship of artists, sportsmen and Jewish people. He saw this as a 'a denial of freedom' which had 'nothing in common with socialism'.[37]

Scargill's career in the NUM also seems to have been an important influence on his decision to leave the YCL. Scargill was now starting to have some success in branch elections: 'the CP insisted I should work in a certain way when I became a trade union official. They wanted me to sell the *Daily Worker* and promote CP ideals through the pit branch of the NUM. I resented this. It meant I wouldn't be exercising all my efforts for the men as miners.'[38]

Some have suggested that Scargill broke with the Communists because he saw that membership would do no good for his career in the NUM, especially at that time when Yorkshire was controlled by the Right. It may be significant that, in March 1961, his branch wrote to the NUM area leadership calling for all Communists to be expelled from NUM membership – a sign in itself of how right wing his branch was at that time. This would have placed Scargill in a very difficult position. And by now Scargill was coming to an accommodation with Elijah Benn, the main right-winger who ran the Woolley branch. They later became firm friends.

It seems there may also have been personal differences between Scargill and local Communist officials. Frank Watters, who had become a close friend of Scargill, had gone to live in Doncaster, but if he had remained in Barnsley at this time, Scargill's departure might have been delayed or prevented.

In recent years Scargill has frequently said that he was never a 'Communist'. What he means by this is that he only belonged to the Young Communist League and was never a member of the Communist Party itself. On a number of occasions Scargill has felt the need to stress this distinction, even though the difference may not mean much to outsiders.[39]

Three leading Communist officials who knew him at that time all express surprise when they learn that Scargill was never actually a Party member. According to Jimmy Reid, all members of the YCL National Committee were expected to join the Party. Frank Watters remembers that Scargill regularly attended Party meetings. Furthermore he had even stood as a Communist in a local election, and it should be noted that he was asked to sell the Party paper, the *Daily Worker*, rather than simply the YCL paper, *Challenge*.

It is also interesting to speculate why in these circumstances Scargill never actually joined the Communist Party. One explanation may be that in the 1950s and early 1960s the question of Party membership was a highly delicate matter. What cannot be doubted in Scargill's case are his strong links with the Party at that time. Perhaps the most interesting aspect of the whole affair is Scargill's *forcefulness* in insisting that he was never a Party member.

Many Party members feel that Scargill's seven years in the Young Communist League provided him with an excellent political education and training. As a leading YCL member he regularly attended Communist Party schools and education courses. The political experience he acquired with the Communists would have been far more rigorous than any he could have gained by being active in the Labour Party. This was all the more important in that Scargill had left school at fifteen and did not have the benefit of a university education. On top of that, he had managed to establish numerous political contacts and friendships with people who would be useful to him in the future.

In making his decision to leave, Scargill was illustrating his independence as a politician. It it wasn't until four years later that he actually joined the Labour Party.

For several years after his first election to the NUM branch committee Scargill annually stood for the post of branch delegate. Even though Woolley was a very right-wing branch, it had elected a left-wing delegate in the late 1950s – Jim Conway, who was a member of the Communist Party. But, nevertheless, the Right had done their best to get rid of Conway, and he was eventually defeated.

Scargill had not been convinced at first that branch delegate was the job to go for. He knew it was local Communist policy for the best people to go for delegates' jobs, but initially he found the idea of standing for secretary more attractive. Frank Watters recalls: 'I told Arthur there wasn't much point in being king of your own men. "You will only get known throughout the coalfield by your contributions as a delegate in the Area Council." '[40]

Scargill stood unsuccessfully for branch delegate several times. One year, to try to ensure against ballot-rigging, he stayed up all night in the Woolley NUM office to make certain that the ballot box wasn't removed. In 1964, he was finally elected to the job he had long wanted. But it was a difficult position when the branch's other leaders were right wing: 'I came to an amicable understanding with them – I went along with the majority decisions at the pit, and they were content to let me speak for them on the area council.'[41]

The other branch officials probably underestimated the importance of the delegate's job. Scargill didn't. Later he would argue that 'branch delegate is the most important position in the miners' union ... It's the position that carries the political authority in the union. The delegate is the man who attends all meetings of the branch, he is the man who comes to the Area Council meetings, which is the *government* of the union, and he is the man who takes the policy decisions back to the branch and takes the policy decisions of the branch back to the Area Council. So it is a very powerful position.'[42]

For Arthur Scargill this was probably the most important election of his career. It enabled him to break free from the narrow confines of his right-wing NUM branch and make a greater impact within the whole Yorkshire area, where he soon joined other left-wingers who opposed their union leadership.

As Woolley's delegate, he was able to make his first impact in the union at a national level too. His first speech at an NUM national conference came in February 1966, at a Special Conference called to discuss the Labour Government's fuel policy. In a short, three-minute speech Scargill accused the NUM Executive of acquiescing in the Government's policy of running down the coal industry. He called for an annual output of 200 million tons, and argued against the closure of 'uneconomic pits' – his words were all very similar to what he has been saying to this day.

But it was his two speeches at the NUM Annual Conference in the Winter Gardens at Eastbourne in July the following year which really started to establish Scargill within the NUM. In the first he argued for extra payments for miners who had to work unsocial shifts, and attacked the then Labour Minister of Fuel and Power, Richard Marsh, denouncing his speech the previous day as 'flannel'.

His second speech, on the situation in the coal industry, would again not be out of place today. He attacked the pit closure programme, but in contrast to the arguments he uses today he maintained that, unless confidence was restored to the industry, young people would carry on leaving in their thousands. The speech made a big impact among the delegates. Scargill was beginning to establish himself within the NUM Left.

Shortly after this period the NUM Secretary, Lawrence Daly, was having a drink with Michael Foot, who was then still a back-bench MP. Foot remarked that the miners' union was no longer producing the potential leaders of working-class politics that it had in the past. 'You haven't met Arthur Scargill,' Daly is reported to have said.

Chapter 3

Adventurers and Splinter Groups

The capture of the Yorkshire coalfield by the militant Left had been complete.

– Lord Robens[1]

A few hundred yards north of Barnsley's 1930s Town Hall, just beyond the roundabout, at 2 Huddersfield Road, can be found the headquarters of the Yorkshire miners. It's rather an impressive building, built in 1874, with crenellations and turrets. At the back of the miners' offices is the Yorkshire miners' Council chamber – a large hall, built in 1912, with stained glass windows, busts of former miners' leaders and, above the door at the back, brightly coloured plaster reliefs of underground mining scenes. Ten rows of sturdy oak chairs – a hundred and sixty seats in all – indicate how much larger the Yorkshire coalfield once was: nowadays the delegates barely fill the first four rows. Behind each chair a small drawer contains voting cards for the delegate from each pit. Empty, the large hall has much of the atmosphere of the Debating Chamber of the Oxford Union. But full, the hall is very different.

Here the Yorkshire miners' Area Council meets once a month. The Council is effectively the Parliament and Government of the Yorkshire coalfield, with a delegate from every NUM pit or workshop branch. It is the coalfield's highest decision-making body. In the late 1960s and early 1970s the debates here raged all day, from ten in the morning until five in the evening. Both sides could boast brilliant speakers – Jock Kane, Sammy Taylor and Arthur Scargill, among many others, from the Left, and, on the Right, Jack Smart and Jack Layden (both of whom later became prominent in local government, after failing in the NUM, and succeeded each other as chairmen of the Association of Metropolitan Authorities). The quality of the debates was extremely high, as the rising Left in the coalfield was at last coming to grips with the declining Right.

But at that time, in the mid-1960s, Arthur Scargill was just one member of a group of miners determined to bring about change in the Yorkshire NUM. 'He wasn't that assertive at first,' is one recollection of his initial impact on the Yorkshire Left. The only thing that marked him out was his comparative youth – he was at least ten years younger than any other member of the group. 'In his earlier days he tended to go off at a tangent,' remembers one member, 'and no amount of sound reasoning could persuade him. He wheeled and dealed quite a lot.' Many of the older members saw Scargill as a 'cheeky, young upstart'. Others thought Scargill was too much of a careerist. 'I had reservations about Arthur Scargill's intentions, and about whether he was genuine. I suspected he was a glory-seeker,' remembers one member of the group. 'I was proved wrong.'

Scargill was never very close to any other members of the Yorkshire Left. 'He was always a loner,' Peter Tait recalls. 'There was always a glass window between you and him. He never had a drink with you like Baines or Rigby would. He was always very cool.'[2]

Scargill began to make his mark around 1967 when the Yorkshire Left formed a public body called the Barnsley Miners' Forum. According to one account the Forum was Scargill's idea, and he was its Secretary. The Forum held regular monthly public meetings on Friday evenings at Barnsley Cooperative Hall which were designed for ordinary miners who were not politically committed – hence, there was no mention of politics in the title. The aim was to convert ordinary miners to more left-wing policies, and to increase militancy on issues such as wages and pit closures

The meetings featured leading national left-wing speakers, such as Lawrence Daly, Mick McGahey from Scotland, Emlyn Williams from Wales and Jack Dunn from Kent, and non-miners such as the Labour MP Frank Allaun and Jimmy Reid. The guests were not always limited to the Left – the local MP, Roy Mason, spoke on one occasion. The meetings were advertised around the coalfield, but were not always well attended. One journalist who remembers going to one or two of the early meetings says there were probably only a dozen people present. After a while he stopped going as he didn't think them important.

The Barnsley Miners' Forum was the public face of the Yorkshire Left, which had been meeting secretly for some time. An important motive behind the formation of the Forum was to deflect accusations by the Right about 'secret caucus meetings'. Of course, behind the scenes, the secret caucus meetings continued as before.

At one point in the late 1960s, the Yorkshire Left had discussed who they should support if the Area Presidency of the Yorkshire Area NUM became vacant. There was speculation at that time that Sam Bullough might retire early, especially when he went into hospital to have a kidney removed. Jock Kane and Sammy Taylor were already Financial Secretary and Compensation Agent respectively. and were ruled out by the Left as candidates for tactical reasons: if either man had won the Presidency there was still the risk that the Left would lose the positions they had previously held.

Two candidates emerged from within the group: Jim Oldham, Chairman of the Doncaster panel, and Arthur Scargill. After discussing the matter for virtually the whole of one meeting in the Albert Club, the group decided by a majority of about three to one to go for Oldham. It was not a surprising choice. Scargill was only just thirty; Oldham was nearly twice Scargill's age and had many years' experience. Kane and Taylor were among several older members of the Yorkshire Left who thought Scargill was simply too young for union office, and they personally were cool towards him because he had left the Communist Party. But some members of the group remember that Scargill found it very difficult to forgive those he regarded as friends who had been strong in their support for Oldham – some say he didn't speak to Ron Rigby for a year afterwards. In the event, however, Bullough soldiered on. By the time the job did become vacant, Oldham was sixty-one, and too old to be a viable candidate.

In 1968 the Yorkshire Left and the Barnsley Miners' Forum mounted a major campaign around the Yorkshire coalfield to get the Secretary of the Scottish miners, Lawrence Daly, elected as the new NUM General Secretary. 'We went out and sold Daly to the Yorkshire miners like a packet of cornflakes,' one left-winger remembers. Daly was taken to branch meetings throughout the coalfield, and an invitation was secured for him to address the annual Yorkshire Miners' Gala. The campaign to get Daly elected enabled the Yorkshire Left to be a little more open in their activities and to raise those issues they wanted to put across to the rank-and-file miners.

At the same time a national left-wing group had also begun to meet regularly. Their early work is described in some detail in Vic Allen's book *The Militancy of British Miners*.[3] Allen, who is Professor of the Sociology of Industrial Society at Leeds University, acted as an adviser and confidant for the Left throughout most of this period and helped draw up policy, and to write pamphlets and leaflets. As a member of the Communist Party he had easily won their trust. He had also done research work for some of the left-wing NUM areas.

Until then, the only real national coordination between left-wing miners was organized by the Communist Party. Every year leading Communist miners met for a weekend conference, often in Manchester, to discuss important issues: wages, the piece-work system and any important positions which were coming up for election. Among the key figures who attended were Abe and Alex Moffat from Scotland, Dai Francis from South Wales, Jack Dunn, who was the Kent General Secretary, and Jock Kane and Sammy Taylor from Yorkshire. But the NUM Secretary, Will Paynter, chose not to attend: although he was still a Communist Party member, his links with the Party were weakening.

The new national left grouping was a very important development because it brought together Communists and other left-wingers, and in doing so brought the prospect of the Left cementing together a majority within the union. The new national forum had met for the first time in the County Hotel in Sheffield, two hundred yards from the Midland station, one Saturday in August 1967. The primary purpose of the meeting had been to choose a left-wing candidate to succeed Will Paynter as NUM Secretary. There were about thirty people present, representing the left wing NUM groups in Derbyshire, Kent, Scotland, South Wales and Yorkshire, and the meeting lasted all day. The Yorkshire Left naturally had a strong contingent, which included Arthur Scargill, Ron Rigby and Tommy Mullany. The three people who had coordinated the gathering, following discussions at the NUM Conference in Eastbourne the previous month, were Vic Allen, Bill McLean, who was to succeed Daly as the Scottish Secretary, and Jock Kane, who was elected Chairman of the group.

Lawrence Daly wasn't an automatic choice as the Left candidate. His colleague Mick McGahey, also from Scotland, was another strong contender, but the consensus of the meeting was eventually for Daly because he had made a strong impact at the Eastbourne conference the month before.

After the Sheffield meeting the Left met regularly, and the numbers involved gradually increased. The group consisted of full-time officials and working branch officials. Some areas, such as Kent, actually paid for their own representatives to attend, while others had to find their own expenses. But often the full-time officials would help subsidize the travelling costs of the others. Once established, the national Miners' Forum, as it became known to some people, took on much of the political and organizational role previously assumed by the Communist Party. The Party stopped holding separate caucus meetings – perhaps it is significant that after this time Communist influence in the NUM slowly declined.

The establishment of the national Miners' Forum was a key event in the history of the NUM. Its first tangible success was the election of Lawrence Daly as NUM Secretary. He beat the Lancashire miners' Secretary, Joe Gormley, who later became NUM President. The Forum has carried on meeting to this day, and has approved a single left-wing candidate for each of the major NUM positions contested since then. Jock Kane continued to chair and convene the meetings and, when he retired in 1972, the Scottish Secretary, Bill McLean, took on the job. Nowadays, McLean's successor as Scottish Secretary, Eric Clarke, who also sits on the Labour Party National Executive, acts as convenor.

In the Yorkshire coalfield, left-wingers found they were getting more support for their policies from the men in the pits. By 1967 most of the obvious candidates for pit closure – the most unprofitable mines in Scotland, South Wales and the North East – had gone. Now mines in Yorkshire were threatened. The problem was made worse by the relatively much higher rate of unemployment in the late 1960s, especially in the outlying regions. (Though by today's standards unemployment levels were still very low.)

Yorkshire, being a relatively prosperous area, didn't really start to suffer from closures on a large scale until the mid-1960s. At the same time thousands of the men now working in the Yorkshire coalfield had themselves been transferred from the more militant areas of Scotland, the North East and South Wales. Many of them helped provide the coalfield with a new left-wing ingredient. They were already imbued with the greater militancy of the areas they had come from, but the fact that their previous pits had closed hardened their determination and sharpened their politics.

Another important cause of discontent for the Yorkshire miners was the National Power Loading Agreement (NPLA), signed in 1966 and implemented over the following five years. The Agreement unified miners' wages for the first time throughout all the Coal Board areas. Nationally the Left saw the NPLA as essential to cement together the various areas of the union, which were divided area by area simply by the fact that miners in different areas and at different pits earned different rates of pay. In such circumstances it had been difficult for the Left to secure a unified union. The local settlement of wages and piece-rates meant that power lay with the area leaderships and with the NUM officials at individual collieries. This partly explains why there were so many local disputes and unofficial strikes and yet no strikes nationally.

The architect of the National Power Loading Agreement was the NUM Secretary, Will Paynter. He knew that the unification of wage rates would mean some miners taking cuts in pay but saw it as a vital step if the NUM was to become a strong, unified, national union. In Yorkshire, the NPLA meant wage cuts of almost a third for some miners, but left-wingers were happy to accept these because they believed in the principle of a unified wages structure. But at the same time the Left knew the NPLA would contribute to the overall discontent of miners in the area.

The NPLA was sold on the theory that if prosperous areas took wage cuts, the money saved might help keep open pits due for closure in the poorer areas. But the pay cuts came at a time when all miners were having their pay held back by the incomes policy imposed by the Wilson Government. And the fact was that over the years miners' wage rates had fallen badly behind other industries. Many miners' leaders felt that accepting lower real rates of pay would help to reduce the number of pit closures, simply by reducing the costs of loss-making pits. But the closures continued, and at a rapid rate in 1968 and 1969. The result was that, in Yorkshire particularly, by the late 1960s, miners felt more militant than for a long time. And when local women bus conductors won a pay award of £18 a week minimum, the Yorkshire miners were particularly angry, since it was much more than the minimum wage of NUM members.

The miners had held high hopes that the Labour Government would pursue a fuel policy that would end the series of pit closures and redundancies. But Labour pursued the closure policy just as vigorously as the previous Conservative government, pinning its hopes on North Sea gas and nuclear power. The miners were particularly disappointed because it was a Labour government which was carrying out the closure programme, but at the same time their loyalty to Labour made them particularly reluctant to take industrial action.

The important turning-point for the Yorkshire area, and indeed for the union as a whole, came in 1969. The strike in October of that year became known as the 'October Revolution'. According to Andrew Taylor, the 1969 strike, and the one which followed it in 1970, 'were as much against

NUM policies and leadership since 1947 as against the National Coal Board'.[4]

On paper, the 1969 strike was about the question of the hours of work for those NUM members who worked on the surface rather than underground. Officially, surface workers did an eight-hour day, though for some men it was often 8¼ hours plus mealtimes. Miners underground only worked 7¾ hours. The 1968 NUM Conference called for surface workers' hours to be reduced to 7¼ a day, but by October 1969 the NUM Executive and the Coal Board had done little about it. Meanwhile, feelings among the members about the issue, and about pay in general, were building up, particularly in Yorkshire and South Wales. The miners were encouraged by the recent successful strike by dustmen which had won them a large pay increase.

The Left had long wanted a strike, and saw surface workers' hours as a good issue. They pressed the matter in the Yorkshire Area Council. On 11 October, when the Council heard that, at its latest meeting, the NEC had referred the matter back, Arthur Scargill moved the motion for strike action. After Sam Bullough had been voted out of the chair, it was passed by eighty-five votes to three. Two days later the strike began: all but one pit in Yorkshire struck, and that came out the following day.

The strike was attacked by the NUM leadership. The union President, Sir Sidney Ford, said he was 'absolutely certain that unofficial action will solve nothing and could well prevent the NCB making any further concessions on surface hours'.[5] Lawrence Daly, too, called on the strikers to return to work, even though in Yorkshire the strike was being led by the very men who had campaigned for his election the year before. His reputation on the Left never really recovered after that, and, when he went to Yorkshire a few weeks later and argued that the strike was against the union rules, Daly was denounced as a 'traitor'.

From Yorkshire the strike quickly spread to Scotland, South Wales, Derbyshire, Kent, Nottinghamshire and the Midlands. At its peak it involved 130,000 miners at 140 pits.

In Yorkshire the strike was being led by the miners from the Yorkshire Left. The President and General Secretary of the Yorkshire area, Sam Bullough and Sid Schofield, who opposed the strike, were both by-passed. From a room above the White Hart Hotel in Barnsley, a favourite haunt of miners, the left-wing leaders organized the strike in Yorkshire and beyond.

According to Arthur Scargill: 'We formed an unofficial strike committee, representing the four areas in the Yorkshire coalfield: North Yorkshire, Barnsley, Doncaster and South Yorkshire. And the first thing that we did was to ask ourselves, first of all, was every pit in Yorkshire out? And the answer then "yes". That was completely sewn up. Now what was the next step? Then the next step was to get out every other pit in Britain if we could ... We decided that the best way that we could produce an effective stoppage was to have a rapid mobile picket. We'd used this before in the Yorkshire coalfield, but on a very limited scale and *never* in an organised way. We launched from the coalfield here squads of cars, minibuses and buses, all directed onto pre-determined targets, with five, six, seven-hundred miners at a time.'[6]

The era of the flying picket had undoubtedly begun The 1969 strike was the first time that the tactic was used on such a wide scale.

It is a matter of dispute where and when the tactic of flying pickets actually originated. Any left-wing Yorkshire branch official worth his salt will claim he was the first to use the tactic. Flying pickets had been used by Yorkshire miners in the 1955 and 1961 unofficial strikes. As more and more miners bought their own cars the tactic became more feasible.

Because the 1969 strike was unofficial, those on strike had to get the rest out by themselves. The Left developed the 'domino strategy'. First they picketed out other pits in Yorkshire, then the flying pickets were sent to other coalfields – Derbyshire and Nottinghamshire. At one point eleven Notts pits were picketed out. On one occasion some pickets from Grimethorpe took their racing pigeons with them, and let them fly back to Yorkshire. But the picketing didn't always work, and in Nottinghamshire the Yorkshiremen encountered a lot of resentment. On one occasion the Notts miners brought along their wives to counter the Yorkshire pickets. The following day the Yorkshiremen brought along their wives as well.

The day-to-day organization was on a panel basis, with the Doncaster and Barnsley panels particularly prominent. The Yorkshire Strike Committee, chaired by Jim Oldham, was based on the existing structures of the panels. Between them the strike organizers managed to mobilize several thousand miners to take part in the flying pickets. Later they saw these men as a mass base from which to launch their assault on the Yorkshire area leadership.

The 1969 strike only lasted two weeks – and it is a matter of opinion whether it was successful or not. On the question of surface hours, the

Coal Board would not move. An eight-man delegation of strikers from the Yorkshire Strike Committee went to the TUC General Secretary, Vic Feather, in London. Among the delegation was Arthur Scargill, who was particularly worried that the men would go back with no tangible results from the strike, and was concerned that men were slowly drifting back. Feather agreed to arrange an independent inquiry and the strike was called off.

More important though, shortly after the strike began, the Coal Board had conceded the NUM's 1969 wage claim in full. The Board Chairman, Lord Robens, claimed that the NCB intended to do this anyway, but it is difficult to believe. It was unprecedented for a claim to be met in full, and not surprisingly the strikers believed they had been responsible.

But 1969 was probably most important because it got so many Yorkshire miners used to the idea of going on strike again. And for the first time the Left in Yorkshire had coordinated their action with the Left in other coalfields. As Arthur Scargill insisted later: 'I don't care who the historian is but if he regards '69 as anything other than a complete victory, it's time that he went and did some more thinking about it. Because '69 was responsible for producing all the victories that were to come.'[7]

Even though the strike had to be called off when some miners started drifting back to work, the strike leaders saw it as a moral victory. Not only had their wage claim been met in full, but, perhaps more important, the strike had helped to make the coalfield more militant. The Chairman of the Coal Board, Lord Robens, argued that Yorkshire had now been totally captured by the Left.

After the unofficial 1969 strike the Left also stepped up its other activities among rank-and-file miners. Leaflets and pamphlets were distributed to try to get across the Left's position on the major issues. 'We were deliberately creating a "cadre" force in our own pits,' recalls Jimmy Miller.[8] 'It was a mass education campaign,' says one Yorkshire Left member, Ron Rigby. 'We educated the rank-and-file. People were fed up.'[9] The idea of politically educating miners was not totally new: the right-wing leader of the Durham miners, Sam Watson, in the 1950s held political Sunday seminars to 'educate' members in a different way.

By this time the Left were coordinating nationally over which areas should submit resolutions on which subjects to the NUM Conference. This was to ensure that areas didn't waste motions by submitting them on the same thing. It was agreed that Yorkshire would look after wages.

And in 1970 the new militancy of the Yorkshire miners was seen for the first time on the agenda of the NUM national conference. The area submitted a resolution calling for a basic weekly wage of £30 for face workers, £22 for other men underground and £20 for surface workers. The idea of stating specific amounts was also agreed by the Left, and was designed to replace ineffective motions put forward in the past calling for 'substantial' increases. The Yorkshire motion had originated from Arthur Scargill's pit, Woolley. (This wasn't spontaneous – the Yorkshire Left had previously agreed to leave the wages motion to Scargill and Woolley.) That year the Yorkshire Area Council had decided that their motions should be moved by rank-and-file delegates, rather than by full-time officials, so appropriately it was Arthur Scargill who moved what was the most important motion of the week, saying:

The miners have stood aghast at recent examples of increases obtained in other industries. They have witnessed the dustbin men gain a substantial increase in wages, the dockers, seamen, and more recently the doctors.

Failure to get this wage increase in full will result in my opinion, in thousands of men leaving the coalmining industry. Failure to get this demand, I suggest to this Conference, will release an anger that will make last October look like a Sunday school picnic. No longer will our membership accept that a small increase is better than none. They are fed up with being asked not to rock the boat. We have been told to remain passive. We have remained passive since 1956 and what has it got us? Half the coalmining industry has been obliterated in Great Britain. If this is what passiveness brings us, then we want none of it.

... Let the Coal Board be warned. The miners last October showed that they have been passive long enough, and I suggest to this Conference that if we have people in splinter groups who are going on adventurous paths for £20, £22, and £30, then I am proud to associate myself with them.[10]

Scargill's reference to 'splinter groups' and 'adventurous paths' was a reply to the opening address by Sid Schofield, the President of Yorkshire, who was also acting NUM President. He had warned the Conference:

We must not allow the minority, who are already holding unofficial meetings, to formulate policies that undermine the whole concept of Trade Unionism ... I am quite satisfied that the minorities in our Union, who are arranging unofficial meetings, printing and issuing pamphlets, ignoring the policies agreed upon at Annual Conference, have a purpose in mind to try to undermine the status of Area and National Officials of our Union, and to incite our members into taking unconstitutional action ... believe me, Delegates, there is a real danger that, unless our Union defends itself against these adventurers, then the men whom we represent will suffer. My only concern is for the members and their families. They must not be stampeded into taking action against their wishes; be prepared.[11]

Seconding Arthur Scargill's motion was Peter Heathfield, a full-time official from Derbyshire; and Mick McGahey spoke third. Fifteen years later the three men would be running the union together.

The motion was passed, along with another motion from South Wales proposing strike action if the claim was not met. But, in the first national ballot in NUM history, members voted by only 55 per cent to 45 for strike action, though in Yorkshire the 'Yes' vote was 62 per cent. It was a majority, but not the two-thirds majority required under NUM Rule 43 at that time.

Yorkshire was naturally angry, both with the ballot result and the fact that the National Executive then accepted a slightly improved pay offer. Gradually though, Yorkshire pits came out on strike, led by the Doncaster panel, which sent pickets to collieries in the rest of the coalfield. At its peak the strike affected most of Yorkshire.

Arthur Scargill found his own pit, Woolley, something of an embarrassment in 1970. The branch voted to come out early on, but after a few days many of the men went back, at a time when most other Yorkshire pits were still out. The arguments at Woolley were bitter, as hundreds of pickets gathered outside the pit entrance. Some men complained they didn't want to join the night-shift through fear of having their cars attacked. Woolley had long had a right-wing reputation, but Sammy Taylor later remarked to Scargill that he could hardly expect to get the Left's support for the Area Presidency if he couldn't get his own men out.

At times, the frustrations and anger of some of the strikers in 1970 turned into nastiness and violence, with scenes very similar to those in 1984. Before one National Executive Committee meeting at the NUM headquarters in Euston Road, several hundred pickets from Scotland, South Wales and Yorkshire had gathered outside. The Nottinghamshire Secretary, Albert Martin, and the Lancashire Secretary, Joe Gormley, were attacked as they went through the front door, along with the Vice-President, Sid Schofield, and the meeting had to be delayed for Schofield to recover. In characteristic style, Gormley warned the Scottish miners' President, Mick McGahey, that, if he didn't keep his Scots under control,

Gormley would bring a few dozen Lancashire lads down 'and we'll sort the bloody lot of you out'.[12] Afterwards the NUM Secretary, Lawrence Daly, was unable to leave the building because of the protesters outside, many of whom had only two years earlier campaigned for his election.

Soon the men in Yorkshire drifted back. Like the strike the year before, the 1970 dispute was a failure, at least on paper. But the Left didn't see it that way, and Arthur Scargill felt it had one important political impact: 'the pressure on the right wing was so intense that they saw that if they did not do something about the rules of the union for calling a strike, the left and the rank and file would sweep them aside and there would be an alternative leadership'.[13]

NUM Rule 43 was changed at the 1971 NUM Conference to make a 55 per cent instead of a two-thirds vote in favour sufficient to allow strike action. In Scargill's opinion: 'This was to be the most decisive change of rule ever in the history of the union.'[14]

The 1969 and 1970 strikes had enabled the Left to practise the kind of tactics that were to prove so successful later. The disputes had largely originated in Yorkshire, first with motions from the area which changed union policy, and then with the initiative being taken in strike action. Scargill says: 'After the '69 and '70 disputes it was clear that the union was never, ever going to be the same again.'[15]

Although the Left were now effectively in control of the Yorkshire area, the right-wing leaders still remained in office. But both the President, Sam Bullough, and the General Secretary, Sid Schofield, were seriously ill and could not be expected to stay in office much longer. A sign of the new militancy of the Yorkshire coalfield came in the election for a new national NUM President to succeed Sid Ford, in 1971. The favourite was Joe Gormley, the Lancashire miners' Secretary, who had been beaten for the NUM Secretaryship in 1968. Gormley was on the Right, but, sensing perhaps the new spirit of the times, he was calling for the miners to be the best paid group of workers. The Left's choice, the Scottish NUM President, Mick McGahey, was a mistake in the circumstances. He had been Scottish President for only a year and was still relatively unknown to miners in other coalfields. McGahey was further handicapped by the fact that the NUM Secretary, Lawrence Daly, was also a left-wing Scot – an important factor in a national union which has always had to balance the interests of the different areas and different political factions. Gormley was elected by 117,663 votes to 92,883, but, significantly, in Yorkshire, where Gormley had campaigned hard, McGahey won by a small margin.

By then, the group of left-wingers who had originally begun by meeting secretly in hotels and clubs had effectively managed to transform the Yorkshire NUM.

The Albert Club closed down in 1983: the building is still there but its windows are boarded up. The Yorkshire Left still meets – at a new venue. But very few of the original members attend any more.

Of the two father-figures, Sammy Taylor died in 1971 and Jock Kane in 1977. Tommy Mullany retired in 1979 and served as a Doncaster councillor until his death in 1984. Ron Rigby and Don Baines continued to play an active role in union affairs until the 1980s, but then both took early retirement and are now full-time members of Barnsley Council: Rigby is Labour Deputy Leader and Baines has been Chief Whip, and was Mayor in 1984. Jim Oldham lives in retirement in Thurnscoe, having himself served as Mayor in 1974. He suffers from 70 per cent pneumoconiosis. Peter Tait served for several years on the NUM Executive, but eventually moved to London to become Secretary of the Miners' International Federation. Only Owen Briscoe became a union official, and is still General Secretary of the Yorkshire NUM.

Of those who joined the group later, Jimmy Miller returned to Fife in 1977. His son, David, succeeded him as Secretary at Kellingley (and in the 1984 strike showed he had inherited his father's television skills). Ian Ferguson also returned to Scotland for a while, but came back to Yorkshire and is again branch secretary at Yorkshire Main. Mick Welsh served on Doncaster Council and was elected MP for Don Valley in 1979 and Doncaster North in 1983. Martin Redmond became chairman of the Doncaster panel in 1975, and also served on Doncaster Council, becoming leader in 1982. He succeeded Welsh as MP for Don Valley in 1983.

Vic Allen has said: 'Arthur Scargill selects himself for attention because of his later achievements but in the early days of the campaign it would have been difficult to identify the future leadership pattern in Yorkshire because the field was so rich with talent.'[16]

But Scargill had several things in his favour. First, his charisma, his great ability for self-promotion and his understanding of the importance of television. After the 1969 and 1970 disputes he began to appear on television regularly, and quickly appreciated the importance of the medium. Says the Labour MP Austin Mitchell, who was then a reporter with Yorkshire Television: 'Yorkshire Television created Arthur Scargill.

He was just the voice of the articulate left-wing Yorkshire miner that we wanted. It was our Barnsley stringer who put us on to him but if he hadn't I think we would have had to invent him.'[17]

In contrast, many of Scargill's colleagues didn't think television important, and some felt Scargill was too much of a self-publicist. One colleague from the Yorkshire Left remembers how Scargill would carefully arrange to record an interview for one local television channel in advance, and then do the other channel live. Scargill understood that if he kept his answers short, he would be asked more questions. Everything would be dropped to do television. This television work enabled Scargill to get around the obstacles placed in his way by the right-wing leadership of his area, and it did a great deal to get him known to ordinary rank-and-file miners, who knew nothing of what the Left were doing behind the scenes. And at that stage Scargill was by no means as publicly critical of television as he is today.

Second, Scargill was still remarkably young. Most of the others in the Yorkshire Left were at least ten years older than Scargill, and his chief rival, Jim Oldham, was twenty-seven years older. Few were young enough to follow the same career path to the top of the union, even if they had wanted to. Arthur Scargill had time on his side.

He also had luck, a burning ambition, and what one colleague calls 'a cunning instinct for being in the right place at the right time'.

Chapter 4

The Battle of Saltley Gate

We took the view that we were in a class war. We were not playing cricket on the village green, like they did in '26.

– Arthur Scargill on the 1972 strike[1]

In December 1983 Arthur Scargill appeared on TV-am to tell viewers of the three 'magic moments' of his life. The first was VE Day in 1945 when he was only seven years old, and the second a school visit to the Festival of Britain in 1951 when he was thirteen. Both were patriotic occasions, and, for Scargill, no doubt the same could be said of his third and most memorable 'magic moment'. This was in February 1972, during the miners' strike, when he and several thousand pickets succeeded in closing Saltley Coke Works in Birmingham. For Scargill it was 'the greatest moment of my life'.[2]

The Battle of Saltley Gate, which symbolized the miners' historic victory in 1972, has become part of trade union mythology, and part of the mythology of Arthur Scargill. When Scargill became President of the Yorkshire miners he hung a painting in his Barnsley office portraying the events at Saltley, with himself prominently in the foreground.

And yet there are very conflicting accounts of Saltley, and of the role played by certain individuals that week in February 1972. While historians grapple with what really happened in badly documented events which occurred hundreds or thousands of years ago, it is tragic that it should also be so difficult to determine what really occurred only a few years ago, under the full spotlight of television and the press. Newspaper and television accounts are superficial. Personal memories are already fading or have become heavily tarnished by vanity and political considerations. A complete account of Saltley may never be told.

The 1972 strike was the most important of the NUM's two battles in the early 1970s, though both resulted in major victories for the union. When the 1972 strike was concluded, a few days after Saltley, the miners had obtained nearly all their original demands, and achieved a 27 per cent pay rise.

The 1972 dispute was the natural consequence of the unofficial strikes of 1969 and 1970. At the 1971 NUM Conference Yorkshire proposed a similar wages resolution to the one the same area had successfully moved the year before. It called for specific minimum wages of £35 for face workers, £28 for other underground workers and £26 for surface workers. Just as in 1970, the motion originated from Arthur Scargill's branch, Woolley. But, because it wasn't Scargill's turn to be a delegate to the national conference in 1971, he was unable to propose the motion himself. Nevertheless, the resolution was passed unanimously and the Conference agreed to consult the membership over industrial action if the Coal Board didn't meet the union's claim. The same conference had also changed the union's rules so that industrial action could be taken with a 55 per cent rather than a two-thirds vote in favour, and because of this a national strike now looked a definite possibility.

After negotiations the Board rejected the NUM claim, and a new Special Conference implemented a ballot on strike action and started an overtime ban.

The Left felt that an overtime ban would serve a number of useful purposes. First, it would help reduce coal stocks because essential maintenance work would have to be carried out during normal time instead of at weekends. That would hinder production. Second, by reducing wages, it was thought the ban would make members more militant and more willing to take strike action if the ban was seen not to work. This was a tactic which would be used again, notably in 1973–4 and 1983–4.

Accordingly, when the ballot was held at the end of November, there was a 58·8 per cent vote for a strike (which would actually have been a 'No' vote under the old rules). The first national coal strike since 1926 began more than a month later, on 9 January, after further talks with the Board, and amid much press speculation that the miners would easily be beaten. It was several generations since the miners had won a strike.

At first, the NUM leadership seemed to have little idea about how the strike would be conducted. 'They hadn't a clue,' Scargill said later.[3] Nevertheless, the canteen in the basement of the NUM headquarters in Euston Road was turned into a national strike centre.

In Yorkshire the miners began by picketing their own collieries, and the tactic of sending pickets to other locations evolved only gradually. One of the first outside sites to be picketed was the Coalite plant at Grimethorpe, where dozens of lorries were to be seen coming out loaded with coke.

Within a day or two, Don Baines sent pickets from his own branch, Brierley, to the plant. They were soon joined by men from Peter Tait's branch, Grimethorpe, a few hundred yards up the road. Soon Baines agreed a permit system with the plant management, which meant that lorries for hospitals and old people would be allowed through, provided they had a permit signed by the NUM. The system was later adopted elsewhere, and soon dozens of lorries could be seen queuing up each day on the street outside the Yorkshire NUM headquarters, waiting for permits.

Like the national leaders, the Yorkshire area leadership had little experience of running strikes, nor had they much enthusiasm for it. It was not long before the strike was being run almost entirely by the men who did have such experience and enthusiasm – the Yorkshire Left. The four Yorkshire panels – Barnsley, Doncaster, South Yorkshire and North Yorkshire – each formed an area strike committee, and each set up its own individual headquarters. The Barnsley panel hired a room in the White Hart Hotel, as they had in 1969. They had asked for a room at the Yorkshire area headquarters in the town, but were told it would be unfair on the other panels if they were allowed to have one, a decision which caused some resentment. Most of the coordination of Barnsley strike work was carried out by Baines and Tait, who were Secretary and Chairman respectively, of the Barnsley panel at that time.

Scargill later told *New Left Review* that he was the spokesman for the Barnsley Strike Committee, and that he had also been put in charge of picketing, but Baines and Tait don't remember it quite like that. The Yorkshire Left had just chosen Scargill to be their candidate for the job of Compensation Agent, which had been vacant since Sammy Taylor's death, late in 1971. The Left was therefore concerned that Scargill should receive as much public exposure as possible, especially television coverage, so as to get him well known among the Yorkshire miners. Baines and Tait say in separate accounts that Scargill in fact spent most of his time travelling around Yorkshire and the rest of the country, addressing meetings to rally support, raising money, and giving interviews. According to them, Scargill spent very little time in the Barnsley strike office, and they argue that they themselves coordinated most of the picketing.

The picket at the Grimethorpe Coalite plant got some good coverage on local and national television within only a day or two. Consequently, when Scargill saw this, he rang Don Baines and suggested that he ought to visit the picket to get himself involved in the publicity. Scargill turned up the following day, but then quickly moved on to help set up another picket in Barnsley itself.

The tactic of using flying pickets, practised fairly successfully in 1969 and 1970, was used more and more as the strike went on. 'Points of energy' were the target. Says Scargill: 'We had to declare *war* on them and the only way you could declare war was to attack the vulnerable points ... the power stations, the coke depots, the coal depots, the points of supply.'[4]

They tried to organize the Barnsley pickets as in a military operation. A map on the wall of the strike centre located all the major power stations and coal depots. Local coach firms were kept on alert, ready to carry pickets to wherever they were needed. And log-books recorded any coal movements, the location of all pickets and any incoming telephone messages. But many of those involved say that the operation was far less well organized than people have claimed since.

For the first week operations were confined to the Barnsley area, but late in the week Don Baines got a phone call from the Yorkshire General Secretary, Sid Schofield, who was playing a more active role than has been suggested. Baines was told that the NUM nationally had decided to use pickets to stop coal movements right across the country, and that each mining area was being allocated a non-mining area to look after. Yorkshire had been given East Anglia. Schofield asked Baines to get down to Norwich as soon as possible. He gave him a 'contact' there, and said he needn't worry about money. 'Sid was most emphatic about it. To be frank, I wasn't too enthusiastic. And I'd never been to Norwich in my life before.'[5]

But Baines and four colleagues quickly left for Norwich, where they met Schofield's 'contact', a lecturer at the university, who turned out to be a member of a Trotskyist group, the International Socialists. (Had Schofield known he would have been horrified.) Within a few days the Barnsley pickets had an office – provided by the local agricultural workers' union – and hundreds of pickets began coming down by coach from Barnsley each week. Meanwhile Baines returned to Barnsley to coordinate things from there, leaving Ron Rigby in Norwich.

At first the men in East Anglia were split up across the area, picketing several different sites at the same time, but with little success. Arthur Scargill was among those who argued from an early stage that the men should be concentrated on one place at a time, so as not to spread resources too thinly. This tactic was soon adopted, and according to Scargill's account: 'I picked the 'phone up and called East Anglia HQ and said "Move everything in onto Ipswich dock, move everything we can." We produced a thousand pickets in an hour-and-a-half on Ipswich dock, and stopped the dock in an hour. We left a token picket at the docks, moved on, and closed down the power stations one by one. Within two days we'd shut the whole of East Anglia.'[6]

The pickets in East Anglia were billeted with sympathetic students and lecturers at the universities of Essex and East Anglia. Neither the students nor the miners really knew what had hit them. 'Some of our boys were very comfortable there. We had difficulty in getting them home,' Scargill recalled.[7]

Ron Rigby remembers that the atmosphere between the police and pickets in 1972 was totally different from that in 1984. 'We had very good relations with the police. We met the Chief Superintendent every day, and I told him where every picket was.'[8]

Within a few weeks the Yorkshire pickets believed that they had East Anglia sewn up. But it was not all success for the Yorkshire pickets. Rigby remembers one day receiving a phone call from the Thames area control room, informing him that a lorry-load of coal was heading towards East Anglia: 'I sent a bus-load to follow this lorry. They found it, and followed it for twenty miles. Then I received a phone call: "Ron, you've just sent us on a wild-goose chase. Remember that lorry you sent us to look for? It was carrying sugar beet." '[9]

But very little coal seemed to be moving. Other NUM areas had achieved similar success elsewhere. The miners' strategy was quickly beginning to bite and power cuts loomed for the first time since 1947. The only place the miners seemed to have overlooked was a coke depot near the centre of Birmingham.

On Thursday 3 February a report appeared on page thirteen of the *Birmingham Evening Mail*, headlined 'The Long, Long Queue to Load with Coke'. It was about the mountain of 100,000 tons of coke at a Gas Board coking plant in Saltley, about a mile from the city centre. Thirty thousand tons had been taken away by lorry already. The article said that 650–700 lorries a day were arriving at the depot to buy coke – 'Britain's last major coke stockpile'. Photos in the paper showed queues of lorries about a mile long, and other pictures showed that the trucks came from all over the country, from as far away as Cornwall. One Bolton lorry driver was quoted as saying of the miners: 'I'm amazed they haven't started picketing it already.'[10]

The NUM had been worried about the coke coming out of Saltley for about two weeks. The then Secretary of the Midlands NUM, Jack Lally, a right-winger, says that long before Scargill arrived he had been liaising with the Gas Board and the police to try to stop the coke coming out of the depot. In other places Lally had quite easily come to arrangements with the police about coal movements, but when he tried to contact the Chief Constable of the West Midlands, Sir Derrick Capper, he got no response.

Shortly after the *Birmingham Evening Mail* article appeared, Lally decided to mount a picket on Saltley, and he was assisted by Roy Ottey, General Secretary of the NUM Power Group. But Lally was short of pickets, since the Midlands is a relatively small area, and most of his men were already assigned to other locations.

The initial, small picket met with little success. The lorry drivers seemed to be carrying on a fiddle with the permit system, by passing permits from driver to driver. Lally himself was almost run over when he tried to photograph a 20 ton lorry rushing into the depot. Lally had warned that he might have to call for reinforcements: 'If necessary, I will bring down 300 pickets from Yorkshire to stop this exploitation at the miners' expense.'[11] At one point Roy Ottey *did* ring Sid Schofield in Yorkshire to ask for reinforcements, but got no response.

That Saturday, 5 February, Saltley was picketed by a handful of men from Hem Heath Colliery in Staffordshire, and from Nottinghamshire.

The Barnsley strike office had heard about Saltley early on Saturday afternoon. Peter Tait argued that nothing should be done about it until the strike committee met on Monday morning, because nothing would be happening at Saltley over the weekend. But Scargill wanted to do something straight away. Messages went out from Barnsley to the local NUM branches for pickets to go to Birmingham, and coaches were arranged to carry them. Four coach-loads of pickets were sent from Barnsley, but according to Don Baines, they were back within a few hours.

Baines, who was in the Barnsley office that day, says that the men had gone to Saltley, decided there was no problem there, and so had turned round and come back. Worse still, the pickets had now gone home. And, on one of the coaches, the picket coordinator had already paid his men their picketing money for several days in advance – and hadn't dared to ask for it back when they returned.

Scargill was furious, and immediately set about sending more coaches to Birmingham, and arranging accommodation for the men for when they got there. So who could it be more appropriate to ring than his old friend Frank Watters, who had moved to Birmingham in 1967 to become Communist Party District Secretary. Watters had in fact been working on Saltley for two or three days already, and, had liaised well with Jack Lally, even though politically they were poles apart. He had visited the depot the day before and had tried to get more pickets from the local trades council. Watters had also arranged an appeal for pickets at an Irish civil-rights rally in Birmingham that Saturday to mark the events of Bloody Sunday, which had happened a few days earlier.

Scargill told Watters he would be sending 200 men in coaches straight away that evening, and another 200 later that night.

'The biggest headache was this,' Watters says. 'What do you do with 400 men on a Saturday night? I thought he was mad. When I said he was mad, he says "Comrade, you asked for them. I'm delivering them." Bed and breakfast, look after them. And then, of course, early morning, Scargill arrives, like the general. His army now had arrived. I got them bedded, looked after with a few pints.'[12]

Watters went to the Star Social Club, which is part of the Communist Party headquarters, and found many of the club's customers were willing to take miners home. Other men slept on the floor at the Club, under blankets provided by the Salvation Army. The following morning, at six o'clock, they all went down to Saltley, where Scargill saw what the fuss was all about: 'I have never seen anything like it in my life. It was like the most gigantic stack of any colliery that I'd ever seen. It was estimated that there were a million tons; it was like a mountain. This was no coke depot in the accepted sense. It was an Eldorado of coke. There were a thousand lorries a day going in and you can imagine the reaction of our boys, fresh from the successes in East Anglia, fresh from the successes in Yorkshire.'[13]

That first day, Sunday, Scargill's men – joined by several dozen Irish civil-rights protesters – achieved success. When he rang Barnsley late that morning it was to tell them that the management had agreed to suspend the movement of coal, but that they would start moving it again the following morning, Monday.

In spite of Scargill's arrival, Jack Lally continued to work on Saltley. It was a difficult position for Lally, since, as Midlands N U M Secretary, Saltley was officially his patch, while Scargill was at that time only a branch delegate in Yorkshire. For the next few days both Scargill and Lally helped to organize things, and each believed that he was effectively in charge. It appears that Scargill mainly ran the picketing on the ground – that was the impression the police and the media had – while Lally concerned himself with trying to organize negotiations behind the scenes with the police and the Gas Board. Both men did liaise with Frank Watters though, and Lally agreed to pay him for the food and accommodation Watters fixed up.

Every day that week pickets and police battled with each other – though much of the hostilities involved no more than vigorous shoving on both sides. By Monday evening the local paper had dubbed the picket the 'Battle of Saltley'.[14] But the police insisted that the plant should be kept open and every day that week more and more miners arrived at Saltley from all over the country – including large numbers from South Wales, Scotland and Kent. But Scargill found it difficult to get more reinforcements from Yorkshire, largely, he thinks, because of the right-wing leadership there.

Each day Scargill would command the picket operations, aided by a team of lieutenants. Using a loud-hailer Scargill would encourage his men to heave one way, and then suddenly to apply the pressure from a different angle. He shouted out regular encouragement: 'We've got them on the run lads, they can only last half an hour now.' But he kept in contact with the police, trying to get them to close the depot, but was reluctant to meet any of their requests.

Scargill and Watters soon realized they would need help from other unions. So, on Tuesday evening, Scargill made a forty-minute speech to the East District Committee of the AUEW. 'We don't want your pound notes,' Scargill told the AUEW. He asked them for physical support: 'Will you go down in history as the working class in Birmingham who stood by while the miners were battered or will you become immortal? I do not ask you – I *demand* that you come out on strike.'[15]

Meanwhile, Frank Watters used his contacts in the area to get the other major unions to help, and other leading pickets went to appeal to smaller union meetings in local factories. At the same time local shop stewards visited Saltley to see the picket for themselves.

As the week progressed, fewer and fewer lorries were managing to leave the depot. Things finally came to a head on the Thursday, as Arthur Scargill described later: 'Some of the lads were feeling the effects and were a bit dispirited that no reinforcements were coming. And then over this hill came a banner and I've never seen in my life as many people following a banner. As far as the eye could see it was just a mass of people marching towards Saltley. There was a huge roar and from the other side of the hill they were coming the other way. They were coming from five directions ... and our lads were just jumping up in the air with emotion – a fantastic situation.'[16]

That morning the TGWU and AUEW had called sympathy strikes. Tens of thousands of Birmingham trade-unionists took the day off work, and about 10,000 marched on the coking depot. They arrived at Nechells Place from all sides. One contingent even turned up with a Scots piper at its head. The roads all around the depot were jammed, and the police, with only 800 men, were surrounded and simply couldn't cope. 'Close the gates, close the gates,' the crowd chanted.

At about ten forty-five on that Thursday morning, an official from the Gas Board walked across the yard, took a key from his pocket, and locked the padlock on the gates of Saltley. It is said that some Yorkshire miners were in tears. 'They almost kissed us,' recalls Chief-Superintendent Arthur Brannigan, 'any ill-feeling there was immediately disappeared.'[17]

After the gates were closed, the police asked Scargill if he could now disperse the crowd. He said 'Yes' – if he could borrow their public address system – ''cos mine's knackered'. Standing on top of a public urinal he addressed the multitude: 'This will go down in trade union history. It will also go down in history as the Battle of Saltley Gate. The working people have united in a mass stand.'[18] 'All that I ever stood for in the British trade union movement suddenly came to a head,' he told the television cameras. 'The trade-unionists of Birmingham proved a point that once they stood solidly together, nothing can move them.'[19]

The miners at Saltley would never have succeeded without considerable help from the rest of the labour movement, as Scargill was the first to acknowledge. 'The picket line didn't close Saltley, what happened was that the working class closed Saltley,' he later told *New Left Review*.[20] Both the Communist and Labour parties had handed over their social clubs, and even the right-wing Labour MP and former Gaitskellite Denis Howell helped prepare food for the miners – a sign of the breadth of support they had.[21] The TGWU sent a van with 800 hot steak-and-kidney pies – some of which ended up as missiles. But above all the local unions sent pickets – *en masse*. The era of the mass picket had begun.

At the time Saltley was thought of as a very violent episode. Thirty people were injured, including sixteen policemen, and 180 pickets were arrested, including Scargill himself. But in comparison with recent episodes – Grunwick, Warrington and the 1984 coal dispute – it was a relatively peaceful occasion. The pickets came to an understanding with the police that only one gate would be used, and when police were injured the pushing and shoving stopped, to enable the injured to be carried away.

Scargill's own presence there, and the way he treated the picket like a military operation, was partly responsible for this. Watters particularly remembers how Scargill was determined to keep the men disciplined: 'On the Monday some lads were having a drink, in picket time. This meant they were coming out of the pub at three o'clock, and these were the ones that were doing all the shouting, and Scargill made it quite clear on the Monday night, over at the Star Social Club, he told them, "Under no circumstances do you leave the picket line without the authority. The food's been provided, transport's been provided, but you don't drink during the day. You can do what you like now at night, but when you're on the picket line, you're getting paid and you're there to picket, not to socialize or to drink." And that there in my opinion had a tremendous effect on the kind of discipline that was required for the rest of the week.'[22]

The miners were also fortunate in that the Gas Board did not try to reopen the plant after that Thursday. Arthur Brannigan says they only closed the gates because no lorries wanted to go in that day: 'At the time I said there was no reason why the gates couldn't have opened again the following day. The unions couldn't have arranged the same kind of demonstration. And we could have got more men there by then.'[23]

But the next day, Friday 11 February, the police in fact arranged for Jack Lally to meet the West Midlands Gas Board Chairman, David Beavis, and it was agreed that Saltley would be closed to all but needy cases – hospitals, old people and schools. But the fact was that by then the 100,000 tons of coke had been reduced to 20,000 tons. According to Beavis: 'we were already considering closing the plant before the Thursday, and limiting the supply to priority customers. It was a hollow victory for the miners as far as I was concerned. In fact, by the end of the strike, all the coke had gone anyway.'[24]

Had the Gas Board instead chosen to reopen the plant after the Thursday, the pickets might not have been so successful, and Saltley might not have come to occupy such a glorious position in trade union history. As it is, Saltley has come to mark the beginning of the end of the 1972 strike. The day after, 11 February, Douglas Hurd, who was then the Political Secretary to the Prime Minister, Edward Heath, wrote in his diary, 'The Government now wandering vainly over battlefield looking for someone to surrender to – and being massacred all the time.'[25]

It may not have been coincidental that the day before the gates at Saltley closed the Government called a State of Emergency and appointed a Court of Inquiry under Lord Wilberforce to look into the miners' case. When it reported eight days later, Wilberforce concluded that 'the miners' claim should be given exceptional national treatment', and recommended increases averaging 27 per cent. But the NUM Executive, sensing they could squeeze yet more out of the Government, rejected the proposals. It took a visit by the Executive to Downing Street finally to get the miners back. The miners knew the Government was in a very weak position and started asking for all sorts of other improvements. The Government couldn't grant them fast enough, and Trevor Bell, the NUM Head of Industrial Relations, remembers 'racking my brains' to think of yet more things to ask for.[26]

Within the space of a few days Scargill had become a national figure. Throughout the week he had been the obvious object of attention for the television cameras, and he came out with the sort of lines they were looking for.

Scargill had been appearing on local television for several years, but in the ITN film archives the first reference to him comes on the Tuesday of Saltley. The card in the index reads: 'Mid-Shot. Man shouts abuse at cameraman.' In typical fashion, Scargill was trying to get the TV crew to film a picket who had been injured by a lorry.

Scargill was now the most famous miner in Yorkshire. 'Saltley was the making of Arthur,' says George Wilkinson. 'I told him "You've got to be at the forefront, lad," and he went where angels fear to tread.'[27]

But some NUM branch officials, both in Yorkshire and elsewhere, feel that Scargill's role at Saltley and in the 1972 strike as a whole has been exaggerated. One official says: 'Don Baines and Ron Rigby were heavily involved as well, and the Barnsley committee did a lot to organize picketing.'

Saltley also had a profound effect on Scargill's political outlook. According to Watters, speaking in 1984: 'Saltley made Arthur the leader he is today. The lesson of Saltley is quite clear to him today; it is that mass picketing and the determination of the pickets, will win this strike.'[28]

In Yorkshire the left-wing picket leaders were buoyant, and none more so than Arthur Scargill. Scargill had been chosen as the Left's candidate for Compensation Agent before the strike began, but now, after the strike, he was certain to win. In June he polled 28,050 votes – far more than his two right-wing opponents combined: Jack Smart, who got 9,824, and Tom Roebuck, who got 8,336. When Jock Kane retired as Yorkshire Financial Secretary later in 1972, Scargill took his place on the National Executive.

The Right in Yorkshire had been in disarray for several years, and had never recovered from the time in 1969 when Sid Schofield successfully challenged Sam Bullough for the NUM Vice-Presidency and split their forces in the coalfield. Now, perhaps sensing that their dominance was in danger, they started to organize themselves. After Scargill's victory in the election for the job of Compensation Agent, the Right formed a group called the Yorkshire Association of Labour Miners, specifically designed, they said, to counter the work of the Barnsley Miners' Forum. Chaired by the North Yorkshire NUM Agent, Jack Smart, the group consisted mostly of right-wing NUM branch officials, many of whom were also Labour councillors. One of its stated objectives was to 'oppose any form of totalitarianism or undemocratic creed or action'.[29] Its rules forbade membership to anyone who, in the opinion of the association's Executive, belonged to or was associated with any organization proscribed by the Labour Party – Communists, in other words. The group said it would publish newspapers and leaflets and, perhaps noting Scargill's excellent use of the medium, it volunteered to 'appear on television'. But even though Joe Gormley agreed to address one of the association's initial meetings, its work made little difference to the onward march of the Yorkshire Left. One reason might have been that the Left was receiving information from a member inside the group.

The period following the 1972 strike was one of rapid change within the Yorkshire area, as four officials went within the course of little more than a year. The President, Sam Bullough, died in January 1973, and again Scargill was the obvious left-wing candidate for the succession. His main right-wing opponents were Jack Leigh, who was the Yorkshire NUM Vice-President, and Jack Layden from South Yorkshire. Bullough and Schofield had been ill for a long time and Scargill had frequently had to stand in for both of them. His job as Compensation Agent also gave him an excellent opportunity to shine in an administrative capacity.

In March 1973, at Lofthouse Colliery near Wakefield, seven men died when a coal-cutter broke through into Victorian underground workings and water suddenly flooded in. Scargill devoted all his energies to the case. He spent six days at the mine, going underground regularly with the rescue teams, and keeping relatives in touch. And when Edward Heath visited the pit, he asked to be taken round by Scargill. For the subsequent inquiry Scargill gathered his evidence thoroughly, travelling around the coalfield for several weeks. He went to the Institute of Geological Sciences in Leeds and found old notebooks giving details of underground workings carried out in the nineteenth century. During the two-week hearing Scargill carefully cross-examined each of the witnesses, acting just like a barrister in a court of law. Each day, details of Scargill's questioning at the inquiry appeared in the local and national press. Scargill established that the disaster could have been avoided had the Coal Board taken notice of information available in old archives.

The inquiry hearings took place at the end of May – the very time when the elections were being held for the Yorkshire Presidency, and the publicity about the hearing must only have helped to increase his popularity. Within less than a year as Compensation Agent he had established his administrative abilities throughout the coalfield. But Scargill hardly needed the extra votes. He polled even better than he had for the Compensation Agent's position. Scargill got 28,362, Layden 7,981 and Leigh 7,126 votes. That autumn, an election was held to replace Sid Schofield, who had retired because of his health, as General Secretary. Owen Briscoe was the victor, though with a less handsome majority than Scargill, but still with more votes than the two main right-wing challengers combined. With Scargill and Briscoe holding the two main positions in Yorkshire, and with the Communist Peter Tait, from Grimethorpe, joining them on the Executive, the transformation of Yorkshire was complete.

The Left's victories in Yorkshire had a profound effect on the NUM nationally, just as the Left had planned. On the National Executive Joe Gormley still had a small majority, but it was only small and had to be kept solid. By late 1973 there were eleven members of the Executive who usually voted together and could be described as on the Left. Six were Communists: their public leader, Mick McGahey, the Scottish miners' leader; Bill McLean, Secretary of the Scottish miners and convenor of the national Miners' Forum; Joe Whelan, Secretary of the normally right-wing

Nottingham area; Dai Francis, Secretary of the South Wales miners; and two rank-and-file Executive members – Jack Collins from Kent and Peter Tait from Yorkshire.

Joining them were a comparatively new phenomenon on the NEC, Labour left-wingers, none of whom had been on the Executive before 1971. As well as Arthur Scargill, this group included Owen Briscoe, the Yorkshire Secretary; Peter Heathfield, the Derbyshire Secretary; Emlyn Williams, the South Wales President, and Eric Clarke, from Scotland.

Between them this group provided a new, radical force in NUM politics. And in the NUM Conference the Left's position was even more promising – with probably a small majority over the Right. This was illustrated by the Vice-Presidential election at the 1973 Conference in Inverness, when Mick McGahey beat Len Clarke, the right-wing President of the Nottingham miners, by 155 votes to 126. As McGahey noted just before the famous 1974 strike: 'The fundamental change that has taken place in the mining industry is the unity of the Labour Left and the Communist Party.'[30]

The 1974 strike is the miners' dispute which people remember, simply because it led to a general election and the downfall of a government, but within the history of the miners' union it is less important than 1972.

At their 1973 Annual Conference the NUM had formulated a wage claim of £35 a week for surface workers, £40 for underground workers and £45 for face workers. The same pattern of events was followed as in 1972. The Board rejected the offer and an overtime ban began in November. Further negotiations followed, and at the start of February miners gave an 81 per cent vote for strike action (Yorkshire voted more than 90 per cent in favour).

When Edward Heath called a general election, there were attempts to call the strike off which had the support of Joe Gormley but only five other members of the Executive. The strike went ahead, but with little of the fervour and excitement of 1972. The national leadership was concerned not to lose Labour votes and to keep operations disciplined. Operations were far better organized than in 1972, and more centralized from London. Yorkshire again looked after East Anglia, using the same maps and contacts as it had used in 1972. Only this time there were none of the problems of a reluctant leadership. Now Arthur Scargill was able to oversee the picketing operations from the President's chair.

The biggest picket by the Yorkshire miners in 1974 was at British Steel's

Anchor steel works in Scunthorpe – a new target not touched in 1972. Even before the strike there had been the possibility of a steel shortage, and Scargill hoped that effective picketing, and help from the train drivers' union ASLEF and the steel union, would stop all coal going into the plant. The picket was largely successful and peaceful.

Since 1972 the laws on picketing had been clarified, and the police had taken steps to set up a special operations room at Scotland Yard to help combat flying pickets. But there were no Saltleys in 1974. The NUM was concerned that violent picket-line scenes on television might easily lose the Labour Party votes in the General Election. So the NUM Executive decided to limit the number of pickets at each site to six. (Six years later, the Conservative Employment Secretary, James Prior, was to use the NUM's 1974 limit of six pickets as the basis for his own guidelines which accompanied the 1980 Employment Act.

When the Labour Party returned to power, against expectations, and with fewer votes than the Tories, they had little choice but to agree to most of the NUM's demands. Face workers received the full claim of £45 a week, with other underground workers getting £36 and surface workers £32, together with various other items.

The miners didn't *win* the 1974 strike – the Government lost it. Edward Heath called an unnecessary general election. But 1974 is the miners' strike that people remember and the events of that year gave the miners an aura of invincibility. People believed the miners had the power to topple governments, and naturally associated with that power were the main militant members of the NUM, Mick McGahey and Arthur Scargill.

Scargill argued that Heath need never have called a general election. The previous November the NUM Executive had gone to Downing Street to argue their case and to try to avoid the looming confrontation. Scargill told *New Left Review* in 1975: 'I produced statistics to Heath in Downing Street in the Cabinet room, proving that the calculations that the Coal Board had made and that the Government had accepted were wrong ... Whatever the reason, which is now history, they ignored these arguments ... Eventually, of course, the Pay Board proved conclusively that the calculations we made were right. Had Heath accepted them, he would still be Prime Minister today.'[31]

Chapter 5

Camelot

Ask for the miners' offices, and if they don't know that, just ask for Camelot.

– Arthur Scargill to journalist, November 1974[1]

Installed in his new job in Barnsley, Arthur Scargill was in a powerful position. At thirty-five, he was the youngest-ever President of the Yorkshire NUM. He was seen as one of the men responsible for the miners' victories in the strikes of 1972 and 1974. In his own area the Left were now in control of the Executive and Area Council and held the two most important full-time positions. Scargill had rapidly become one of the best-known trade-unionists in Britain: much in demand as an interviewee and a hate-figure for the right-wing popular press. In October 1974 *Harpers and Queen* magazine tipped him as one of the names of the future, along with Jack Straw and William Waldegrave. Scargill lunched with the editor of *The Times*, appeared as a guest on Michael Parkinson's Saturday night chat-show, gave seminars and lectures in universities and was a regular panellist on *Any Questions*. He became a favourite speaker among the middle-class undergraduates of the Oxford and Cambridge Unions. He found it difficult to turn any invitation down.

With a long career still ahead of him Scargill could also hope to achieve even higher office within the NUM. Indeed, shortly after he became Yorkshire President, a further move upwards looked possible. The NUM Secretary, Lawrence Daly, was ill and it looked as if he might have to resign. Mick McGahey would probably have won the Left's nomination to succeed Daly at that point, but Scargill might then have become Vice-President in McGahey's place. At times Scargill seemed to give the impression that he was running the NUM already – on one occasion he personally offered on television to implement a national productivity scheme for an experimental six-month period.

Scargill's style at the Yorkshire NUM was totally different from that of the traditional working-class trade union leader. 'King Arthur' wore neat pin-striped suits, took great care over his personal appearance and drove around in smart cars. His image was more that of a young business executive, going places. The Yorkshire office was modernized and refurbished. Its twenty-year-old office typewriters were replaced with up-to-date equipment. His own office was lined with wood-panelling and recarpeted. Scargill worked phenomenally hard, turning up at eight o'clock every morning before the rest of his staff and generally not leaving the office until late in the evening.

When Arthur Scargill took over the Yorkshire Presidency, it was agreed that he should continue with his old job as Compensation Agent. The national union, which pays the salaries of all area officials, was looking to save money, and told Yorkshire it would have to reduce the number of full-time area officials from five to four. Combining both jobs seemed the best solution, since it meant no official had to be made redundant and it avoided the risk of a right-winger winning the position. The Yorkshire NUM did protest, but Scargill personally was not displeased. For him, keeping the Compensation Agent's job turned out to be a shrewd move.

Scargill has frequently said that if he had not been a miner and trade union official he would have liked to have been a barrister. He would have been very good at the job. As a result of the Lofthouse case, and others, Scargill quickly became known as 'the miners' QC' (a title once also given to Sir Stafford Cripps). Indeed, Scargill is thought to have provided the model for the miners' union official, Ackroyd, in Barry Hines's television play about a pit disaster, *The Price of Coal*, written in 1975.[2]

One branch official recalls that, before Scargill was Compensation Agent, 'you could wander through the Compensation Department and nobody seemed bothered about anything'. Scargill changed all that, and was particularly proud of the work he did, as his annual reports showed:

In 1972, the year when I took office, I found we had cases on our books going back as far as seven and eight years. It was clearly an unsatisfactory state of affairs and one which could only be put right in time ...

It was essential to establish the general principle that no common law damage case remained on our hands longer than six months, without having an answer either in the affirmative or in the negative ...

To give some idea of the situation I inherited in 1972, it is well to recall the total damages recovered and the average per case.

The total damages recovered was £637,585.55. This represented an average of £619.00 per case.

As a result of the policies introduced at the end of 1972, the position has been transformed dramatically and the results at the end of 1976 vividly demonstrate the success of the policies pursued in the Compensation Department. In 1976, the department settled 1,034 cases which was practically the same as the number settled in 1972. The amount of damages recovered was £1,296,525.00. This worked out on average per case at £1,253.87. This means we have in four years, more than doubled the amount of Compensation, and I consider that this is a splendid record.

It represents in strict percentage terms, over 25 per cent per year increase over the amount recovered in 1972.[5]

It should be remembered that inflation between 1972 and 1976 had been high, and, strictly speaking, judges' notes generally determined the level of compensation awards. But Scargill managed to get the legal costs of each case included in the amount of the award. His record as Compensation Agent was a very good one.

Scargill pursued individual claims with great determination, fired by his own father's health problems (he arranged a full check-up for his father soon after he got the job). Miners were astonished at the way he could remember individual details about their cases. And even when the claim was unsuccessful, miners felt assured that Scargill had at least tried his best.

Every Saturday morning he held a surgery for miners with compensation claims. The machinery of the nine-man Compensation Department was streamlined, with special filing envelopes which could show the state of play on each claim. Past records were held on microfiche. Scargill brought into the department Mick Clapham, a former miner Scargill had known since he was a branch official at Dodworth and who had gone on to university and become a lecturer. (When Scargill became NUM President, Clapham moved with him to become Industrial Relations Officer. He was one of the NUM representatives involved in the negotiations with the Coal Board in 1984.)

Keeping the job of Compensation Agent helped extend Scargill's popularity in Yorkshire. In pursuing the cases so vigorously he won respect from miners who might not agree with his politics. And the job helped him keep in constant touch with branch officials in the local collieries. And he used the 'miners' QC' title in his 1981 election address for NUM President.

On the NUM Executive, though, Scargill was often isolated, even among the Left. He called himself the most hard-line of the hard-line members.

Right-wingers recall that he seemed to oppose nearly anything of any importance Gormley suggested and would often be in a minority of one, or be supported only by the Yorkshire General Secretary, Owen Briscoe. On one occasion the Executive unanimously approved a new government pneumoconiosis scheme. The following month the scheme came up again and this time Scargill was one of only two members to vote against it. 'Why did you vote against me?' he asked Peter Tait in the train on the way home to Yorkshire. Tait explained that he could not see how things had changed from the previous meeting. Scargill proceeded to take a pile of papers from his case and explained that he had legal advice that the scheme was deficient. Tait wanted to know why then he hadn't presented this information before. Another habit Scargill had was to tell other members of the Left they should do as he advised 'because I have it on good authority that . . .' But when the others asked, Scargill would never reveal what his "good authority" was. Many members of the Executive, both Left and Right, found his tactics irritating, and found it difficult to take him seriously.

Scargill would often use the press to his own advantage. As soon as an Executive meeting was over he would be telling reporters his version of what had happened and often denouncing whatever decisions had been taken. His handling of the media became very skilful, as Ian Ross, then BBC television Industrial Correspondent, recalls.

'The practice was that about ten minutes after Executive meetings were over, Joe Gormley would give a press briefing upstairs in the conference room. Scargill knew this. So as soon as the Executive was over he would rush down quickly and, sniffing out a television camera or two, would tell us all his version of what had happened and we'd get his version – and usually his criticism – of what the Executive had decided. That way, he managed almost to set the agenda for the briefing with Joe immediately afterwards. Joe used to get very annoyed about it – quite justifiably sometimes because Scargill's version wasn't always right. Once or twice Joe would say: "If he's given you an interview I'm not going to give you one." '[4]

Joe Gormley kept a firm grip on the Executive, although the Left were strongly critical of his 'wheeler-dealer' politics. With a right-wing majority on the NEC Gormley could normally be sure to get his way, and the evening before each meeting the right-wing majority and the left-wing minority on the NEC held separate caucus meetings to decide their strategy for the following day. The Left would generally meet in the

County Hotel, in Upper Woburn Place. The Right met in the Marquis Cornwallis pub, in the landlord's private sitting-room. These Right caucus meetings – which were more important because the Right formed the majority – were convened by Sid Vincent, who had succeeded Gormley as General Secretary of the Lancashire miners and had run Gormley's campaign for the NUM Presidency. Gormley's other two main 'fixers' were Len Clarke, the President of the Nottingham area, and Les Storey, Secretary of the Colliery Officials and Staffs area. The Right would also meet regularly at Joe Gormley's home in Sunbury-on-Thames.

But occasionally the Right's majority was threatened: a member might be unavoidably absent or mandated by his area to vote differently. In such cases Gormley might use his Presidential powers to rule items out of order, or simply delay a vote until the next meeting. The Left could try to challenge his ruling, but they needed a two-thirds majority on the Executive to succeed. Gormley was very much in charge. On one occasion, Owen Briscoe from Yorkshire told him he ought to get hold of a copy of Citrine's *ABC of Chairmanship*. 'Look, I'm chairing this meeting, not bloody Citrine,' Gormley shot back. Since Scargill became President it has often been said that he has copied many of Gormley's tricks.

As President of the NUM Gormley exercised his powers of patronage very effectively. People he needed for support might be wined and dined lavishly, or he might arrange for them to go on some attractive foreign trip.

Gormley loved meeting and doing deals with Prime Ministers – Conservative or Labour or with Sir Derek Ezra, the Coal Board Chairman. Often the NUM Executive was excluded altogether from negotiations with the Government as Gormley stitched up some deal at Number 10, or at Hobart House, the Coal Board headquarters.

In this he came into his own after the 1974 election. The miners were in a very strong position in relation to the new Labour government, which had come to office partly as a result of the miners' strike. Many miners' leaders had been unhappy with the treatment they had received from the 1964–70 Wilson government, which had presided over the massive pit closure programme, but now the initiative lay with the NUM. In 1972 and 1974 the NUM had shown that it could break any government incomes policy. Labour's new Social Contract therefore depended on the miners. The miners were among the first groups to negotiate in the annual wage round, and year after year it became vitally important for the Government that the miners be seen to settle within the Social Contract.

If the miners were seen to abide by the voluntary wage restraint, it was likely to be respected by the rest of the labour movement.

The new Energy Secretary, Eric Varley, was an NUM-sponsored MP, and at the time of his appointment actually sat on the NUM Executive as one of two Parliamentary representatives. Another NUM-sponsored MP, Alex Eadie, was also an Energy minister. Together, the Labour Government, the NUM and the Coal Board established a good relationship, which produced the famous 1974 'Plan for Coal', which guaranteed the future of the industry. Part of the understanding reached between Joe Gormley and his friends in government was that there would be both wage restraint by the miners and an incentive scheme.

Over the next five years the main opposition to that special relationship came from Arthur Scargill and the Yorkshire miners. During his nine years as President of the Yorkshire NUM Scargill was involved in two major continuing battles with Joe Gormley and the right-wing majority on the NUM Executive – over the introduction of an incentive scheme and over the Labour Government's Social Contract.

At one Executive meeting, in December 1974, Gormley even decided to stay away through illness in order to beat off a left-wing challenge and save the Social Contract. The Executive was due to decide on that year's wages claim. The Left wanted a £30 a week increase, which would have destroyed the Social Contract almost before it had begun. The Right simply wanted to go for a 'substantial' increase, but it looked as if the Right would lose by one vote, because one important right-winger was expected to be absent. So, cleverly, Gormley decided to use his heavy cold as a reason to stay away, and rang into the office to say he couldn't turn up. Gormley had calculated that that would mean the Vice-President, Mick McGahey, would have to take the chair, which would deprive the Left of his vote and win the day for the Right. But McGahey went one better. He applied an old internal NUM rule which said that if an issue had previously been discussed at a sub-committee all the members of that committee were bound to go along with the decision of that committee. That would win the issue for the Left. Right-wingers were furious and walked out. Gormley was quickly telephoned and decided he wasn't too ill to rush into the office to get McGahey's ruling overturned. Once again, Gormley won the day, and the Social Contract remained intact.

Labour Prime Ministers lived in great fear of what the miners might do – the whole future of their economic policy and of the Government depended upon it. By 1975, the Left within the NUM was pressing for a wage claim of £100 a week. The issue would be decided at the NUM Conference in Scarborough in July. The vote would be very close and a nervous Harold Wilson flew to Scarborough to urge moderation. In his memoirs Wilson admits: 'Never, in thirty years in Parliament, had I prepared a speech with such care – dictating, writing, amending, inserting, discarding and drafting again.'[5]

On that occasion at Scarborough the £100 a week claim was dropped after a split on the NUM Left which saw Scargill isolated by Communists in the other areas. Mick McGahey and a Communist caucus had decided that a £100 a week claim would not receive sufficient public support and one or two of them also saw its withdrawal as a way of embarrassing Scargill. Scargill and Yorkshire went along with the £100 demand right until the last minute, even though others on the Left wanted it to be withdrawn. Scargill was eventually forced to support a compromise motion, and in a subsequent ballot miners agreed to the £6 a week increase of the Social Contract. Scargill later described his action, in eventually supporting the compromise and ignoring his mandate from Yorkshire, as his 'greatest regret'.

Scargill quickly learnt he couldn't always count on the rest of the Left. Many of the older, more experienced left-wingers disliked his brash style and his ambition. Some on the Left felt that Scargill had taken too much of the credit for the NUM's victories in 1972 and 1974. It didn't help good relations when the Yorkshire President was reported to have made comments such as 'You're talking to the inventor of the flying picket',[6] since other areas, apart from Yorkshire, had also used the tactic widely. Relations between Scargill and Mick McGahey were particularly bad. On one occasion Scargill laid into McGahey at an NEC meeting for agreeing to a pit closure in Scotland. Privately McGahey was very critical of the Yorkshire leader, and told many people it would not be in the NUM's interests for Scargill to be elected President, and argued that he had to be stopped 'at all costs'.

The differences may have been fuelled and exaggerated by the media. That is certainly Vic Allen's view:

There were personality differences. Arthur Scargill had intruded as an official leader with national importance with the speed of a projectile and had disturbed the fairly settled leadership relations which had been established during the struggles in opposition. Some left wing Area officials were disturbed by the speed of the intrusion. The mantle of unofficial leader which had been borne by Michael McGahey was carried less securely after Scargill became the president of the Yorkshire Area. There were rival left wing contenders for whatever crown in the Union became vacant who were reluctant to resolve their competition in a quiet, informal manner. There were discussions about styles of leadership, contrasting Scargill with McGahey, with rival camps emerging.

Personality differences existed but they were less significant than the ones projected in the media.[7]

The battle over an incentive scheme was linked to the argument about the Social Contract. It was a dispute which dragged on for several years, and which Scargill and the Left eventually lost, with far-reaching consequences for the union and the 1984 strike. And the battle over the scheme was to set important precedents for the future.

A productivity scheme had first been discussed in the early 1970s. While the Coal Board saw it as a means of increasing productivity, certain members of the NUM saw it as a back-door route to higher wages. Joe Gormley also believed that a scheme would help restore the differentials between face workers and other miners, which had been eroded by the introduction of the National Power Loading Agreement and recent pay settlements. The 1972 Wilberforce Report had recommended that such a scheme be negotiated by the end of that year, but no plan could be agreed on.

In 1974 the issue came up again, after the Relativities Report which gave the miners their pay increase had also recommended a productivity deal. The new Labour Government saw a scheme as a way of avoiding embarrassment and conflict over further high pay rises for the miners. In September 1974 the details of such a scheme were hammered out, but without either the National Executive or a Special Conference actually agreeing to them. The issue gave Scargill a national prominence he had not enjoyed since 1972, especially when he and the Yorkshire delegation walked out of the Special Conference in protest. In Yorkshire he campaigned intensely against incentives, and personally designed posters which went around the coalfield depicting a black cross dripping with red blood. The posters warned that the scheme would mean 'more blood on Britain's coal, more deaths, more serious injuries, more pneumoconiosis'. Scargill accused the Coal Board of trying to destroy the NUM: 'It is out to turn the wheel of history backward to the old days of the Miners' Federation when the areas counted for more than the national body.'[8]

The Left won the day. A pithead ballot rejected the scheme with a 61·53 per cent vote against. In Yorkshire the 'No' vote was 83 per cent.

At that point Joe Gormley seemed to accept defeat: 'the NUM membership have had their say at the ballot box and the productivity deal is not on'.[9] But, in spite of what Gormley said, it was not the end of the matter. Joe Gormley and others on the Right saw a productivity scheme as a means of increasing miners' wages without breaching the tight guidelines of the Labour Government's Social Contract, which politically the Right felt obliged to support.

But the Left feared that any such scheme would destroy the unity within the NUM which had been achieved by unifying wages under the NPLA of 1966. They believed (rightly) that it would inevitably reintroduce great differences in pay between the areas and make it harder to achieve solidarity over industrial action in future. The Coal Board may have hoped this too. The Left also argued that any incentive scheme would make miners work frantically hard and thus lead to a vast increase in the number of accidents – the 'blood on the coal' argument.

Not surprisingly, the idea of such a scheme was supported most by those areas which stood to gain most, and where output per man was high – Nottingham and South Derbyshire in particular. Miners in these areas had had to suffer big pay-cuts in real terms as a result of the NPLA.

The scheme was resurrected by the South Derbyshire area at the 1977 Conference in Tynemouth, but rejected by the delegates by just one vote. The Cokemen, who had an incentive scheme themselves, unexpectedly voted against a national scheme. In spite of this, within weeks the National Executive agreed a new scheme with the Coal Board, and it was put to a pithead ballot.

The Kent area went to the High Court to try to stop the ballot going ahead, arguing that it was unconstitutional since the wishes of the NUM Conference were being ignored. But not everybody on the Left approved of going to law. Mick McGahey feared they might lose, and felt that unions should settle their own disputes. But Arthur Scargill was among those who approved of legal action and the Yorkshire area paid Kent's costs. But both the Vice-Chancellor and Lord Denning found in favour of the leadership, and the ballot went ahead.

Before the ballot Scargill again campaigned strongly against the scheme. He argued that miners would be required to make 60 per cent more effort before they earned a penny more – a line which was described as 'totally inaccurate' by the Coal Board. And more posters – this time with coffins – again suggested it would increase the number of mining deaths.

In the event, and against all expectations, the leadership again lost the ballot – but not the fight. The National Executive then gave permission for individual areas to make their own incentive schemes, and argued that unofficial arrangements were already widespread – even in the areas which had opposed a formal productivity scheme.

Again the Left took legal action. Yorkshire, South Wales and Kent took the leadership to court, seeking injunctions against any such local agreements. Again, when it came to law, the Left lost.

Nottingham, South Derbyshire and Leicester were among the first areas to take up the Executive's advice, but it wasn't long before even the left-wing areas had to cave in and agree to their own schemes. Even Yorkshire, which had originally voted three to one against, was forced to negotiate a scheme within a matter of weeks.

Throughout the long battle over incentive schemes both sides of the NUM set precedents in the conduct of the union's internal affairs. Joe Gormley had managed to use the power of the Presidency and the support he had on the Executive to get just what he wanted, in spite of votes against incentive schemes by both the NUM Conference and the membership as a whole. The spirit of the union's rule-book, and arguably the letter (though not according to the judges), was cast aside. Furthermore, the idea of by-passing the wishes of the union nationally by taking action area by area would in turn be used by the Left to bring about the 1984 strike. Equally, in taking legal action and going to court, the Left was itself setting a precedent. In the labour movement it is not normally the done thing to settle internal disputes in the courts. Seven years later, in 1984, the roles would be reversed. The Left would be interpreting the rule-book to its own favour, and working area by area, and the right-wing pro-ballot miners would be going to court. Only, in both cases the judges upheld the position taken by the Right.

The incentive scheme works by giving each pit a standard performance figure for production, assessed jointly by the NCB and the NUM. Once three quarters of the figure has been reached, miners start earning bonuses and there is no limit to how much they can earn in bonus payments. Today, some face workers at Nottinghamshire pits are earning as much as £20 a shift in bonuses, and £50 a week on average. On average nationally, incentive payments account for about 20 per cent of miners' pay. Some miners, however, earn very little in bonus pay-ments.

The productivity scheme did lead to a substantial increase in many miners' wages, but there is little evidence that it has led to an increased number of accidents. But the Left were correct in their fear that it would produce great differences between the amounts of pay earned by miners in different collieries and different coalfields. Since 1977 the productivity scheme has undoubtedly weakened the union as the Left knew it would, and it reintroduced many of the divisions which existed before the NPLA. According to Dave Douglass, a left-wing branch delegate from Hatfield Main in Yorkshire: 'When we had a sliding scale, we had a county union. When we had the NPLA we had a national union. Now with pit-based incentives we have no union at all.'[10]

In Yorkshire, the 'consciousness raising' that the Left had carried out so successfully in the late 1960s and early 1970s continued, with Scargill at the head of the Yorkshire machine. As time went by, right-wing officials in the local branches continued to be replaced by left-wingers. In 1976 Scargill began publication of the *Yorkshire Miner*, a newspaper designed to counter what he saw as the 'propaganda' of the Coal Board's own publication, *Coal News*. He brought in as editor Maurice Jones, a sub-editor on the *Sheffield Morning Telegraph* and a member of the Communist Party. The *Yorkshire Miner* had a popular tabloid approach, was well laid out and had pin-up girls on page three – something which brought strong criticism from feminists. The paper was an important part of the education and information campaign which was gradually transforming the Yorkshire miners into the most militant area in Britain.

In 1977 Scargill and the Yorkshire miners tried to repeat the tactics of Saltley on the picket lines at Grunwick, a mail-order photographic laboratory in north London. A group of Asian workers had walked out on strike demanding the right to join a trade union and recognition for that union. Grunwick became a *cause célèbre* – the 'Ascot of the Left', at which every left-wing group had to be seen. Thousands of pickets came from all over Britain.

The Scottish President, Mick McGahey, was in fact among the first NUM figures to stand outside Grunwick, and actually spoke of 'doing a Saltley'.[11] Miners from Scotland, South Wales and Kent had a strong presence, but it was the Yorkshire area which gave the most support. Hundreds of miners were driven down from Yorkshire in coaches. Each man received £15 a day for loss of pay and £8 subsistence money. On one particular day the Yorkshire area spent £23,000 on such expenses.

The miners were thankful for the support that they had received from other unions in 1972 and 1974. But Roy Grantham and some members of APEX, the union involved at Grunwick, felt that some of the miners were simply trying to flex their muscles with the police. For Scargill the dispute had more important implications: 'We haven't fought for trade union rights for two centuries to give them away in the back streets of Willesden.'[12]

But the police were much better organized than at Saltley and there were far fewer pickets. Not once was the factory closed. Perhaps because of the police success the violence at Grunwick was much worse than anything in 1972. 'There's no comparison,' said one miner. 'I was at Saltley Gates and it was a children's Sunday picnic by the side of this.'[13] 'Up in Yorkshire we say this is 11th business, it's a hob-nailed boot job,' said another. On 21 June 1977 Scargill was arrested outside Grunwick and charged with obstructing the highway and the police. The court found him innocent on both charges after seeing pictures provided by a *Morning Star* photographer.

Another arrested that day was Maurice Jones, editor of the *Yorkshire Miner*. He was charged with insulting behaviour, but after being released on bail Jones suddenly vanished and failed to appear for his court case. He turned up in East Germany a few days later with his wife and young daughter, asking for political asylum. Jones claimed that while being held at Wembley police station by the Special Branch they had produced a thick file on him and threatened his daughter: 'You have a delightful little daughter, Mr Jones, and the roads become very busy at this time of the year.'[14] Jones said the police had told him to make the *Yorkshire Miner* like any other union paper and not to make it 'so dangerously attractive'. They revealed that they had details of his wife, Leena, who is Finnish, and suggested that since she had worked illegally in this country for a hairdresser in 1970 she might be deported.

The police version of events was that Jones had gone 'grey' when asked to give his fingerprints. The suggestion was made that Jones feared his prints would connect him with various political crimes they suggested he had committed in the past.

The tabloid press, and the *Daily Mail* in particular, gave the story big coverage, and it made the front-page headlines in several papers.

Reporters were sent to East Germany to track Jones down and every detail of his past was reported. The story certainly provided good ammunition for the anti-Scargill press.

Eventually Scargill and the Yorkshire General Secretary, Owen Briscoe, flew to East Germany to persuade Jones to return and answer the charge. At Heathrow, Jones was arrested again, and was involved in scuffles with four policemen.

When the case came to trial two months later Jones was convicted of threatening behaviour, fined £50 and ordered to pay £50 costs, and then he was fined a further £50 for failing to answer to his bail. Jones continued to edit the *Yorkshire Miner* until Scargill became NUM President in 1982, when he was appointed editor of the NUM newspaper, *The Miner*.

In 1978 the NUM made a decision which eventually ensured that Scargill would be the Left's candidate to succeed Joe Gormley. The Annual Conference passed a rule-change which meant that nobody could stand for office as a national or area NUM official beyond the age of fifty-five. The rule was changed at a time when the union was pressing for early retirement and Gormley argued: 'You cannot have early retirement schemes for one section of the membership and not others.'[13]

The change was a fairly logical one. The union was also giving people the option of retiring at sixty, but if they had taken up their position beyond the age of fifty-five and then retired at sixty it would mean they had less than the necessary five years of superannuation contributions.

But Gormley must have known what effect the rule-change would have on the NUM's immediate future. Before the rule-change was passed it was highly likely that the Scottish miners' President, Mick McGahey, would have contested the position, either as the Left's only candidate or possibly in competition with Arthur Scargill. In May 1978 McGahey was fifty-three, which now meant he could only be a candidate if Gormley announced his retirement in the next two years, which looked unlikely.

Many right-wingers have not forgiven Gormley for pushing the rule-change through so hastily, since it put McGahey's main rival on the Left, Arthur Scargill, into a commanding position.

The change also had an important effect as far as the Right's candidate for the Presidency was concerned. Les Storey, the General Secretary of the NUM's clerical section, COSA, was due to retire soon and until then the hot favourite to succeed him had been John Varley, the President of

COSA. But under the new rule Varley was now too old. The result was that Trevor Bell, who as head of the NUM's Industrial Relations Department had worked closely with Gormley, was able to succeed Storey as COSA General Secretary, take his place on the NUM Executive, and later become the Right's main candidate to succeed Gormley (originally with Gormley's blessing).

Meanwhile, back in Yorkshire, minds were already considering the succession to Arthur Scargill, in preparation for the time when he went on to higher things. In 1978 the Yorkshire Vice-President, Jack Leigh, retired. Peter Tait, the NUM Secretary at Grimethorpe and one of the original members of the Yorkshire Left, was chosen to be their candidate. The Right's main challenge came from Jack Layden, from Maltby in South Yorkshire. The Left were worried, though, that Layden was a strong candidate, and Arthur Scargill suggested a clever move, which was apparently designed to defeat him. Layden was naturally expected to do well in his own area, South Yorkshire. So, as well as nominating Tait, the Left would put up another left-winger, from South Yorkshire, simply to divert votes away from Layden. The Left's choice for this role was Jack Taylor from Manvers Main.

But Tait was in a weak position at that time. As a member of the National Executive he had been made chairman of a sub-committee on concessionary coal. The committee reached an agreement with the Coal Board which nationally would give miners, and particularly miners' widows, more concessionary coal overall. But the scheme involved a certain amount of equalization, which meant most people in Yorkshire receiving less coal. The proposals of Tait's committee led to a major row in the Yorkshire Left, and Scargill argued that Tait should have negotiated for the Yorkshire miners to keep their coal allocation and for every other area to be brought up to their level. So strongly did Scargill feel about the issue that at one point he organized a joint meeting in Mansfield about it, with the right-wing Nottingham area President, Len Clarke. Relations between Scargill and Tait had never been good: at this point they were very low indeed.

And Jack Taylor turned out to be a much stronger candidate than many people had expected. Taylor not only got more votes than Layden in the first round of voting, but in the final ballot he beat Tait.

Tait felt he had been let down by the Left, some of whom didn't like the fact that he was then a Communist. 'I lost because the machinery wasn't

working properly for me,' he says.[16] Although Arthur Scargill spoke for
Tait at public meetings, the two men did not get on, as had been shown
during the concessionary coal argument.

Soon after his defeat Tait became General Secretary of the Miners'
International Federation, which meant he had to leave the Communist
Party, and his differences with Scargill continued. His NUM career was
over. (It is interesting to note that, apart from Scargill, none of the people
of calibre in the original Yorkshire Left, notably Tait himself, Don Baines
and Ron Rigby, ever made it to full-time office in the NUM.)

Taylor's victory when he wasn't the official Left candidate also says a
lot for his own popularity with the men. The result put him well on the
way to succeeding Scargill as Yorkshire President, where he has since
shown himself to be independent of Scargill.

Scargill not only showed himself to be a clever operator within the
Yorkshire NUM, but during the latter period of his Yorkshire Presidency
he took an increasing interest in affairs within the Labour Party, where
he applied many of the principles of left-wing organization, caucusing and
solidarity, which had proved to be so successful in transforming the
Yorkshire NUM.[17]

The late 1970s were a period of great disillusionment on the Labour
Left, over the record of the Wilson and Callaghan governments. Groups
such as the Labour Coordinating Committee and the Campaign for Labour
Party Democracy (to which the Yorkshire miners were affiliated) were
emerging and challenging the Party leadership and its constitution.

The Labour MPs in the handful of Yorkshire seats which can be
described as mining communities have some of the largest majorities in
the country, and are sponsored by the Yorkshire Area NUM. In those
seats, the NUM has a high proportion of the delegates to each constituency Labour Party General Committee, though rarely a majority.

In the late 1970s it had become apparent to some in the Yorkshire NUM
that the union's influence in these constituencies had been on the decline
over the previous thirty years. The eight NUM MPs in Yorkshire in 1945
had been reduced to five by 1979, and two traditional mining seats,
Castleford and Rother Valley, had been lost to Labour MPs who weren't
miners. This might have been expected with fewer people working in the
coal industry, but Scargill didn't see it like that.

Part of the problem was that the union did not take up its full entitle-
ment of delegates, simply because not enough miners who were Labour

Party members could be found to do the job. Many NUM delegates had a poor attendance record, and furthermore didn't always vote the same way. But what particularly annoyed Scargill was that the Yorkshire-NUM-sponsored MPs were generally on the Right (having been selected in the days of the old regime) and generally had little time for the union's new left-wing policies.

The problem first showed itself in 1975 over the EEC referendum. The Yorkshire NUM Council had declared itself opposed to continued member-ship of the EEC, but four of its five NUM MPs were in favour, and actively campaigned for a 'Yes' vote to stay in the EEC. Angry with this apparent defiance, the Yorkshire Council then called on its MPs who 'accepted Union money' to follow union policy or accept the consequences. The House of Commons Committee of Privileges ruled this to be a breach of Parliamentary privilege, and the NUM Executive had to overrule the Yorkshire NUM. But Scargill had made his point.

Scargill's first move within the Labour Party came after the 1979 election defeat. The union changed its rules on nominating NUM-sponsored candidates so that the Yorkshire NUM Executive drew up the final list of candidates from nominations submitted by the branches. (Previously any candidate nominated by the branches was automatically included on the final list.) Since the Yorkshire NUM Executive was domi-nated by the Left it meant that right-wingers would no longer be selected. Thereafter all new Yorkshire-NUM-sponsored candidates would be on the Left.

The second move, also in 1979, was designed to increase NUM influence within each constituency. The union insisted that all NUM colliery branches must affiliate to *all* constituencies where they had any members at all. With the dispersal of miners over the years, men often lived much further from the pits they worked in, so each NUM branch would have members in several constituencies, and would therefore be entitled to delegates on each constituency general committee. Each branch had to pay a minimum affiliation fee of £5 per constituency, and it was agreed that the Area Political Fund would pay the money itself when an NUM branch couldn't afford it.

The campaign came to a head in Roy Mason's seat, Barnsley, where Scargill and his wife were themselves delegates to the General Committee – Arthur from Woolley NUM, where he had once worked, and Anne from the Worsbrough ward branch. Mason, who had served as Northern

Ireland Secretary in the Callaghan Government, was exactly the kind of Labour MP Scargill didn't like. A former miner, Mason had a generation earlier been a Scargill-style whizz-kid himself, winning the Barnsley nomination in 1953 at the age of twenty-eight, with Communist support and against the wishes of the local Labour establishment.

What particularly annoyed the Yorkshire Left was that Mason, an NUM-sponsored MP, had served as Minister of Power in the late 1960s, during a period when nuclear power was being expanded and dozens of mines were being closed every year. (Scargill's pit, Woolley, had proposed withdrawing financial support from Mason as early as 1967.) Later, under Callaghan, Mason had defended the Government and the Social Contract, at a time when Scargill was saying that Labour would lose the next election and deserved to do so.

Shortly after the 1979 election defeat, a motion came before the Barnsley General Committee proposing that the Party dissociate 'itself from the political attitudes of its MP'. The Yorkshire NUM Executive started to mobilize its delegates in Barnsley, and called a faction meeting of all its delegates to the Barnsley Constituency Labour Party, to decide the NUM line.

Ninety-five delegates turned up for the General Committee meeting that month (normally the attendance was only fifty or sixty). Many of the new faces were from the NUM. Party officials had printed agendas for the usual number of people, but, in what became known as the 'Xerox scandal', it was discovered that the new faces had received their agendas from the NUM, and that they had been photocopied at the Yorkshire NUM headquarters.

A resolution was passed by ninety votes to two, after it had been amended by Worsbrough, to dissociate the Party from the 'views expressed by some [MPs] that Conference decisions should not be binding on a Labour Government'.

At the next General Committee meeting a month later (after another faction meeting), that year's Barnsley Labour conference delegate was mandated to vote for all the left-wing resolutions on Party democracy. Afterwards the constituency chairman, Ronnie Fisher, a Mason supporter, described the NUM delegates as 'political prostitutes': the NUM delegates had each been paid £2.70 to attend their faction meeting, held at the Yorkshire NUM council chamber an hour before the Labour Party meeting took place in the same hall. But this is perfectly legal under the NUM rules, which allow the union to pay members for lost wages or expenses while on union business.

The NUM then stepped up its efforts. It affiliated all retired NUM members through its headquarters branch, which thus increased the HQ representation on the General Committee from one to six. They became known as 'Dad's Army'.

The following January, at the constituency Annual General Meeting, Mason's Barnsley fortress fell. A left-wing slate drawn up by the NUM faction ousted all the right-wing officers of the constituency and only one non-miner remained on the Party's Executive – Jack Brown, a close friend of Scargill. Roy Mason's days as Barnsley's MP seemed numbered. (At one stage it looked as if some of the other right-wing NUM MPs might be threatened too, among them Eddie Wainwright in Dearne Valley, Alec Woodall in Hemsworth and Albert Roberts in Normanton.)

But the campaign against Mason eventually failed, because the Yorkshire miners made an important tactical error. At the time, all the coalfield constituencies were due to be reorganized as a result of boundary changes, so the Area Council decided not to get involved in the first round of selections and reselections, which took place before the boundary changes. The expectation was that once the boundaries had been changed there would be a second full round of selections. In Barnsley, in the first reselection process Roy Mason was opposed only by Jack Brown, the Party Vice-Chairman, who calls himself a 'Stalinist'. The choice posed a dilemma for the miners' faction on the Barnsley General Committee – if they voted for Brown, the left-winger, it would be more difficult to introduce a left-wing NUM nominee the second time round. Scargill himself ended up voting for Mason, because he was a miner, and Mason scraped in by sixty-one votes to fifty-three.

But after the constituencies had been reorganized, it was too late and the second round of selections never took place. The Labour Party decided that sitting MPs should take any new seat upon which they had the major claim. Full-scale selections only took place automatically where the seat was disputed between existing candidates. It meant that the Yorkshire area lost its chance to get rid of the MPs it didn't like. In addition, once Scargill became NUM President in 1982, and went to London, some of his personal drive behind the political campaign was missing.

By the time of the 1983 General Election, most of the right-wingers had survived – Geoffrey Lofthouse in Pontefract and Castleford, Allen McKay in Barnsley West and Penistone, and Peter Hardy in Wentworth. Eddie Wainwright and Albert Roberts both retired. Wainwright was replaced in the Dearne Valley/Barnsley East seat by a left-wing NUM nominee, Terry Patchett, but Roberts's replacement in Normanton was a prominent right-wing miner, William O'Brien, who had opposed Owen Briscoe for the Yorkshire General-Secretaryship in 1973. He wasn't sponsored by the NUM though. Two new seats in the area went to NUM-sponsored left-wingers: Kevin Barron and Martin Redmond became MPs for Rother Valley and Don Valley, respectively. The Yorkshire NUM now has four left-wing-sponsored MPs and can be expected to make further progress as other MPs come up for reselection or retire: it will only be a matter of time before the Yorkshire coalfield is returning a solid block of left-wing Labour MPs to the House of Commons.

Chapter 6

The Road to Cortonwood

> The Prime Minister should not make the same mistake as Ted Heath did in 1974, when he thought he could take us on. The issue about jobs is much more volatile than pay.
>
> – Joe Gormley, February 1981[1]

In January 1981 the Yorkshire NUM held a ballot of its 66,000 members. 'Are you in favour of giving the NUM Yorkshire Area authority to take various forms of industrial action (including strike action, if necessary) to stop the closure of any pit, unless on the grounds of exhaustion?'[2] At the time the ballot was purely a matter of principle. Jack Taylor, Yorkshire Vice-President then, and now President, remembers: 'It was a general view to ballot on the principle of "uneconomic" closures. We needed guidance from the members – to ballot them when there wasn't total media interference. We campaigned carefully.'[3]

It had become clear to leaders of the miners' union that, with the Thatcher Government's economic policy involving tight financial controls on the nationalized industries, the coal industry would be under severe pressure. The 1980 Coal Industry Act required the Coal Board to break even by 1983–4. The Board would be looking to cut costs and that would almost certainly mean a return to the pit closure programmes of the 1960s – closures not on the grounds of exhaustion but of economics.

Arthur Scargill and the area leadership received an overwhelming 86 per cent vote for their appeal. It would be more than three years before the ballot was used to justify industrial action, by which time Scargill would be President of the NUM. The Yorkshire ballot attracted very little attention at the time. It appeared to be a local area matter. The ballot result would be Scargill's legacy to the Yorkshire miners – a time bomb which would tick on for three years.

Only a few days after the Yorkshire ballot, pit closures became a national issue. And, for the third time in less than ten years, the miners would humiliate a Conservative government. It was the only significant occasion on which Mrs Thatcher has been beaten by a trade union.

Early on in February 1981 the NUM met the NCB Chairman, Sir Derek

Ezra, to discuss his plans for the industry in the light of Government cash-limits. The union asked for details of pit closures in the coming year, but Sir Derek said he could not provide them since those announcements were provided by local area directors (a practice introduced in 1958 when the Board wanted to announce fifty-six pit closures at one go). The announcements were due in only a few days, but they were pre-empted by the widespread industrial action which followed the meeting in London between the union and the Coal Board.

There are mixed reports about what exactly happened at that meeting. But NUM leaders emerged talking about fifty pits closing and the loss of 30,000 jobs. (Later the final tally emerged as twenty-three pits and four million tonnes of production – very similar to the 1984 targets.) On the NUM Executive, Right and Left united to pass a unanimous motion giving the Government seven days to bail out the Coal Board and prevent the mass closure of pits. Otherwise, they said, they would order a ballot with a strong recommendation to strike immediately. The degree of unity was remarkable. 'We have never before shown this sort of united front in the mining industry,' said Trevor Bell of COSA.[4]

Amid all the rumours, the action of miners at pit level outpaced even the united Executive. All over Britain miners were stopping work, in defiance of Joe Gormley's advice and the pleas of their own area leaderships to wait for the official go-ahead. It was called the 'snowball' effect as men took action area by area, much as they were to do later, in 1984. Within days of the NUM ultimatum the stage looked set for a complete national strike, with or without a national ballot. South Wales was solid for action. Durham said they would strike if their four pits under threat weren't reprieved. Kent and Scotland looked certain to follow, and in Yorkshire Arthur Scargill said his men would also strike.

Joe Gormley, anxious that any industrial action should be sanctioned by the union rule-book, appealed to miners to 'hold their fire' until after a national ballot. Gormley warned miners that the union could face court action unless they abided by their own rules: 'There are many people in the country today, even members of the union, who have the ability to go to law to make sure that the union does not take action if it is against the rules of the union.'[5] It is an interesting comment, in the light of what was to happen in 1984.

There were marked parallels with 1984. But, unlike 1984, the miners in 1981 received extraordinary pledges of support from other unions –

which never had to be realized. Perhaps most notably, the steelworkers' leader, Bill Sirs, and Sid Weighell of the railwaymen said they could not rule out a general strike if there was a confrontation with the Government. The seamen's union promised 'maximum support' for the miners. So did South Wales transport workers. Within days the 'snowball' had turned into an avalanche.

The Government, which at first held back from the dispute, quickly responded to calls for intervention. Mrs Thatcher made it known she wasn't interested in the 'Who Governs Britain' principle on which Edward Heath had fought the miners in 1974. She and her Energy Secretary, David Howell, tried to assure the Commons that far fewer pits would close than the miners believed. Howell agreed to meet the NUM and the Board together. The original day of the meeting was brought forward as the situation became more urgent.

Then suddenly, almost as quickly as the confrontation began, it was over. At the talks between Ezra, Gormley and Howell, the Government gave in. Gormley emerged to say that the Government had agreed to provide a 'hell of a lot' of money for the coal industry and that there was no need to continue the strike. But unofficial strikes continued in several areas, and men said they would only go back with 'copper-bottomed guarantees'. As the NUM Executive met to recommend a return to work, even Arthur Scargill was jeered by pickets from Kent who accused him of 'not being active enough'. Scargill actually voted against the Executive and initially tried to bring the Yorkshire area out on strike. But, after receiving assurances from Sir Derek Ezra that a South Yorkshire pit, Orgreave, wouldn't close, the strike in the coalfield was 'suspended'. The other left-wing areas soon followed suit.

On television the following Sunday, the Cabinet minister John Biffen admitted that the Government had given in to 'industrial muscle'. But with the benefit of hindsight, perhaps the real showdown had only been postponed.

David Howell agreed in 1984 that the decision to climb down in 1981 had been 'entirely' a tactical one: 'Neither the Government nor I think society as a whole was in a position to get locked into a coal strike ... In those days the stocks weren't so high. I don't think the country was prepared, and the whole NUM and the trade union movement tended to be united all on one side.'[6]

Arthur Scargill told *Marxism Today* that he doubted whether the 1981 confrontation could be regarded as 'a total victory for the miners': 'Talk of victory is premature. The Government sidestepped the issue because they realised they could not win. The miners had an unanswerable case. There was massive public support but most important of all there was trade union support ... it's got to be recognised that the Government merely avoided an actual confrontation.'[7]

That summer, Joe Gormley finally announced his retirement as President of the NUM, and the campaign to succeed him officially got under way.

The succession had been a matter of growing speculation for several years. Gormley had to retire in July 1982 at the latest, but for a long time he had been hinting that he might go earlier. He was determined, however, that the Communist NUM Vice-President, Mick McGahey, shouldn't succeed him, and, as we have seen, it is thought that Gormley wanted to stay in office long enough to prevent McGahey from standing. Certainly, by the time Gormley announced his retirement, McGahey was fifty-six and, under the NUM rules Gormley had himself changed three years earlier, was now too old to be a candidate.

That made Arthur Scargill the obvious choice for the Left, although Peter Heathfield, Secretary of the Derbyshire miners, was another possibility, and could have claimed seniority over Scargill since he had been a full-time area official since 1966. But when the Left met in Birmingham in 1980 to choose their candidate there was little dispute that Scargill was the man. Some left-wingers feared that he would have stood anyway, with or without the Left's approval, and the Left knew that to win they needed Yorkshire fully behind them. And it was generally assumed that Peter Heathfield would go for NUM Secretary when Lawrence Daly retired. The Left managed to patch up whatever differences they had had in the past and rallied behind Scargill. McGahey was the first to pledge his support publicly.

The Right, on the other hand, were in total disarray. Gormley and his allies handled the question of the succession very badly. At a caucus meeting held at Gormley's home in Sunbury-on-Thames in December 1980, one man had emerged with the disorderly blessing of the group, and, apparently, of Gormley – Trevor Bell. But Gormley quickly became fed up with the whole business: 'The following day, that meeting was leaked to the Press, and straight away I had to tell the "moderate" group:

"To hell with it. If we're going to be conducting this discussion in public, then I can't have anything more to do with it."[8]

Bell had recently become Secretary of the NUM Colliery Officials and Staffs Area, thanks to work by Gormley and his close friend Les Storey, the previous COSA General Secretary. Bell and Gormley had worked closely at the NUM headquarters over the years, where Bell had been Head of Industrial Relations since 1967. But several others on the Right supported Bell only with reluctance. At one point it had been expected that the President of the Nottingham area, Ray Chadburn, would lead the anti-Scargill challenge from the Right, and in 1980 Gormley boosted his prospects by using his casting vote to get Chadburn on to the TUC General Council. That would have meant a straight fight between the two biggest areas: Yorkshire and Nottingham. But Chadburn had lost interest early on and in the middle of 1980 had been prepared to back Bell. He wasn't even present at the December caucus, which lost him support. He was also out of favour with others on the Right for abstaining in a recent vote of censure on Mick McGahey, who had been criticizing other members of the NEC in public.

The Nottingham President couldn't decide what to do – in Gormley's words, he had been 'dithering like the original reluctant bride'.[9] For several months after the December meeting he pulled out of the contest altogether in the interests of right-wing unity. Privately he was worried about whether he would be able to get sufficient support from his own area, Nottingham, since the Left had been making steady progress in the area, under the guidance of their Communist General Secretary, Joe Whelan, and many Notts branches were now run by left-wing officials.

Chadburn was later persuaded to rejoin the battle. But soon afterwards, the Nottingham NUM Area Council embarrassed him by voting 15–9 to nominate Scargill for the job (a sign of how much progress the Left had made in the area). In the end Chadburn could secure the nomination of only tiny Cumberland, an area with just one pit and fewer than 1,000 members. Chadburn handled his campaign very badly.

Trevor Bell, on the other hand, was a methodical and solid campaigner, who turned out to be Scargill's only serious rival. Like Scargill, Bell was a Yorkshireman, and like Scargill he had worked in the Barnsley coalfield. He had been an underground craftsman as a young man, working along-side Roy Mason, Barnsley's MP.

After going to university, Bell been appointed head of the NUM's Industrial Relations Department at its London headquarters. It was in this position that he became a member of COSA, which provided him with a convenient route on to the Executive when he became COSA's General Secretary in 1979, only the year before he emerged as Scargill's leading challenger.

Bell also boasted of having compiled the NUM's evidence to the Wilberforce inquiry in 1972, though his opponents accused him of exaggerating his role in this and playing down the work of John Hughes and Roy Moore at the Ruskin College Trade Union Research Unit.

COSA, with 19,000 members at that time, was, and still is, the fourth largest part of the NUM, with members in each coalfield. This did give Bell a certain amount of 'neutrality' between areas. But many on the Right knew that Bell, as a representative of surface workers, would be distrusted by underground men. And, unlike Chadburn and Scargill, Bell had never been a face worker, which is regarded as the toughest job underground. To remind miners that he had once worked underground his election literature was illustrated with photos of him in mining gear. Scargill had no such need to remind the voters of his underground credentials.

Bell's background in COSA also hampered his campaign. Sir Sidney Ford, who had been NUM President between 1960 and 1971, had also come from COSA, and was thought to have been a bad President. Bell campaigned on a 'common sense' ticket, and for a continuation of the policies of Joe Gormley. He said he wanted to stop the miners being used as 'shock troops' in political battles.

But there was another problem for the Right. Unlike the Left, they hadn't learnt the lessons of previous NUM elections: even under the NUM's transferable voting system, too many candidates from one faction can easily weaken that faction's vote and hand victory to the other side. In 1960 four left-wing candidates had opposed three right-wingers. In the first round of voting the Left seemed to have a clear majority, but the transfers of votes diluted the Left's apparent strength and handed victory to Sir Sidney Ford.

The Right ended up with three challengers to Arthur Scargill in 1981: Bell, Chadburn and a candidate almost unknown outside his own area, Bernard Donaghy, President of the North Western area – the Lancashire miners. The Lancashire General Secretary, Sid Vincent, was determined that his area shouldn't nominate Scargill, but, when one of his branches put in a nomination for the Yorkshire leader, he got worried. He thought his area wouldn't agree to back Bell or Chadburn and so suggested nominating Donaghy as a way of avoiding the problem.

For the Right, it had become a 'Stop Scargill at any price' campaign, and was doomed. The right-wing candidates felt inhibited in areas where other right-wingers were standing, and Yorkshire was obviously forbidden territory. Scargill felt no such inhibitions. The media often felt the need to 'balance' Scargill against the three right-wingers and so gave them each a third of the space Scargill was getting. And none of the right-wingers had anything like the resources of the Yorkshire NUM.

None of the right-wing candidates could realistically have hoped to prevent Scargill's victory. Some people say Gormley hadn't thought properly about the question of a successor. Bell wasn't regarded as a miner, Chadburn couldn't make his mind up, and Donaghy was unknown. As a leading, long-standing right-winger on the National Executive says: 'You've always got this problem of personal ambition on the Right. And then there was Chadburn blowing hot and cold all the time – would he stand or wouldn't he ... they didn't have those problems on the Left.'

One theory has it that privately Joe Gormley ended up supporting Scargill, out of exasperation with the three right-wing candidates – he is reported to have remarked privately that Scargill had done enough to earn the job. He and many other right-wingers felt that Scargill would 'mellow' once he'd been elected, just as other left-wing officials had done. Judging by the tone of Gormley's memoirs, *Battered Cherub*, if he did vote for Bell or Chadburn he cannot have done so with much enthusiasm.

Scargill fought a brilliant campaign. At his election hustings he had 'the punch of a knock-out politician and the perkiness of a stand-up comedian', said one *Guardian* journalist, after attending one of Scargill's election rallies.[10]

But Scargill had effectively been fighting his Presidential campaign for years. He secured nominations from twelve NUM areas, including normally right-wing areas such as Durham, Leicester, Midlands and North Wales. Between them the areas represented 200,000 of the NUM's 240,000 members.

Scargill carried out an extensive speaking tour around the country with well-attended meetings in nearly every coalfield, addressing thirty-six public meetings in the last six weeks. The Yorkshire NUM published a pamphlet he had written, *Miners in the Eighties*, which was distributed to every member in Yorkshire, and widely elsewhere. In effect, it was Scargill's manifesto.

His platform was based solidly on those issues which were to be at stake in the 1984 dispute. Scargill pledged to fight the closure of 'uneconomic' pits and to call for strike action if necessary. He also argued that power within the NUM should be moved away from the 'unrepresentative' National Executive and vested in the NUM Conference, which he said was more representative. In 1984 most of the important decisions would be made by sessions of the NUM Conference, not by the Executive.

When the result was announced on 8 December, Scargill had won by an even bigger landslide than predicted. The voting figures were:

Arthur Scargill	138,803	(70.3%)
Trevor Bell	34,075	(17.3%)
Ray Chadburn	17,979	(9.1%)
Bernard Donaghy	6,442	(3.3%)

The Left naturally interpreted the result as a vote of approval by the NUM membership of the policies on which Scargill had fought his campaign. 'It demonstrates that miners are fighting for progressive policies,' said Mick McGahey soon after the result was announced.[11] But despite their landslide vote for Scargill, the NUM membership failed to back Scargill's calls for strike action. Between then and the start of the 1984 strike the NUM membership would vote against a strike on three separate occasions.

The first, in January 1982, took place while Scargill was President-Elect and Gormley still President. It had come about as a result of the breakdown in the pay negotiations the previous month. The NUM was claiming 23·7 per cent, while the Board's final offer was only 9·5 per cent.

Joe Gormley was strongly against strike action, and on the day before the ballot he appealed to miners to reject the advice of his own Executive. Writing in the *Daily Express* he argued: 'I have no false hopes that Maggie Thatcher will cough up for us ... There's not much likelihood of a strike producing more than a few more quid in my judgement.'[12]

The membership voted by 55 per cent to 45 per cent against strike action over their pay claim. In Yorkshire, however, the vote was 66·5 per cent to 33·5 per cent in favour.

Gormley's intervention was probably not the deciding factor, but the

Left naturally blamed him. Mick McGahey said it was 'outrageous' for a President to flout his union's policy so openly. Arthur Scargill called it an 'act of betrayal without parallel in the history of the NUM', and attacked Gormley for using the 'capitalist press'.[13]

Ironically, only a month before Gormley had used the very same newspaper to tell the world he thought Scargill would 'make a good President of the miners' union'.[14] Relations between the two men never recovered after the second article. When Gormley retired three months later, Scargill and ten other members of the Executive boycotted his farewell dinner in Cumbria.

Appropriately, Gormley's departure in April was followed by that of the man he had worked with so closely over the previous ten years, the Coal Board Chairman, Sir Derek Ezra. Ezra's replacement was the Deputy Chairman, Norman Siddall, who was only a 'caretaker', and due to retire in a year. When the NUM Executive met Siddall for the first time, the meeting was over in record time – just three and a half minutes. Scargill had asked Siddall for a copy of the 'hit-list' of pits earmarked for closure. When Siddall said no such list existed, Scargill walked out, followed by all the Executive except Roy Ottey. As Scargill said: 'We didn't have time for a cup of coffee. But I think they got the message.'[15] Norman Siddall said he thought it had been a 'stage-managed' confrontation. Certainly Scargill had warned journalists that they ought to get there on time.

The message was that from now on pit closures would be the main issue. At that year's NUM Conference in Inverness he warned the Board and the Government: 'Under no circumstances shall I countenance a pit closure programme. We shall never again relive the experiences of the '60s and it would be suicidal of the Government or board to think otherwise.'[16]

The second ballot defeat came in October 1982, six months after Scargill had assumed the Presidency. A new round of pay talks had again broken down, and a Special NUM Conference began an overtime ban. For the ballot, Scargill carried out a speaking campaign around the country, trying to generate support for a strike. This time the immediate issue of pay was tied to the question of pit closures, and this time even NUM right-wingers expected a clear majority to vote for a strike.

But they were wrong. The membership voted against more decisively than they had the previous January. The vote was 61 per cent to 39 per cent against strike action. But in Yorkshire the vote was 56 per cent to 44 per cent in favour.

The result came as a shock to everybody. The Kent General Secretary, Jack Collins, warned: 'The same men who have failed to back Scargill over pay will be screaming for him to lead them over jobs.'[17]

As if to tell the NUM membership that they had made a mistake, Scargill revealed immediately that he had documents showing that the NCB intended to close seventy-five pits. A few weeks later the NUM published in The Miner what it claimed was the NCB's 'hit-list' of fifty-five collieries. The NCB accepted that the documents were genuine, but said they had been misinterpreted.

The following March the pit closures issue came to the fore again, this time over the closure of one particular pit – Tymawr Lewis Merthyr, near Pontypridd in South Wales. The South Wales NUM voted to strike and to try to win support from other areas. There were many parallels between the circumstances in March 1983 over Tymawr Lewis Merthyr and the circumstances a year later in March 1984. The Scottish area voted to join South Wales on strike, even though the area had refused to strike over one of their own pits, Kinneil, the previous December. And Yorkshire voted to strike as well – by a vote of seventy-three to two in the Area Council. Jack Taylor, the Area President, said: 'Now is the time to fight. If we sit back and do nothing we can guarantee that within a very short space of time there will be a reduced industry.'[18]

At the same time right-wing areas, Lancashire, Durham and Nottingham, began to arrange ballots, but some right-wing NEC members were voicing disquiet about whether the strike was constitutional. 'I don't think "constitutionality" will be the deciding factor,' answered Mick McGahey.[19]

Arthur Scargill decided the situation was so serious, with different areas taking different courses of action, that he called an emergency meeting of the National Executive. When it met, on 3 March, Scargill argued that it should call a national strike without a national ballot. He proposed doing this under Rule 41 (see Appendix), under which individual areas can call official strikes provided they get them sanctioned at national level. The Right argued that the closure of Lewis Merthyr was linked inextricably to the closure of pits nationally, and so it should be put to a national ballot. And they argued that divided action would lead to a divided union. Their arguments prevailed: it went to a national ballot.

The same argument was to surface a year later – with a rather different outcome.

The ballot produced an identical result to that of the previous October: 61 per cent voted against strike action, with 39 per cent in favour. Yorkshire again went against the national trend, but its 54 per cent pro-strike vote was 2 per cent down on October.

The March ballot had taken place amid strong rumours that the Government would appoint the Chairman of British Steel, Ian MacGregor, as the new Chairman of the Coal Board. 'Waiting in the wings, waiting to chop us to pieces is Yankee steel butcher MacGregor,' wrote Scargill in a special campaigning edition of *The Miner*.[20] But the prospect did nothing to increase miners' militancy, in spite of MacGregor's record at British Steel, where he had taken more than half of the jobs out of the industry. The Government asked Siddall to stay but the Chairman felt his health was not up to it. Eighteen days after the ballot result, Ian MacGregor's appointment was confirmed.

By the summer, with a 141-seat majority behind her, Mrs Thatcher seemed to be preparing for a battle with the miners which looked increasingly inevitable. In the post-election Cabinet reshuffle, Nigel Lawson was replaced at the Department of Energy by Peter Walker, who, as Industry Secretary under Heath, had been involved in the coal disputes of 1972 and 1974. 'Peter, I want you to go to Energy,' Walker is said to have been told by the Prime Minister the day after the election. 'We're going to have a miners' strike.'

But after the three previous ballot defeats the Left had been rethinking their strategy on pit closures. At one point Scargill even suggested a 'big hitter' strategy, whereby certain highly productive pits would strike and their miners would be supported by a levy on those still at work. But that proposal was dropped and emphasis placed on the idea of winning the members' 'hearts and minds', so that next time there was a ballot on pit closures the call for strike action would be supported.

That summer the NUM Conference in Perth unanimously passed an emergency motion instructing the National Executive and national officials 'to immediately embark on a campaign to win the whole-hearted support of Miners not only to oppose pit and works closures, but all reductions in manpower'. The motion also gave the Executive power to conduct a national ballot on the issue 'at a time to be deemed most appropriate'.[21]

Supporting the motion, the Yorkshire President, Jack Taylor, voiced reservations about the idea of striking area by area: 'The N.E.C. must run this battle. We cannot have Areas on their own, we cannot have pits on their own, because when we are divided they will beat us ... We are not going to be a National Union unless we do it together.'[22]

'We must begin a campaign and start a far-reaching educational pro-gramme to win our members wholeheartedly for the fight to defend this industry and their own jobs,' Scargill had told delegates in his opening address. And in the debate on the emergency motion he asked for unity: 'For God's sake, I ask members of our Union to stop knocking COSA, stop knocking the Midlands or Nottinghamshire and start winning them for support for the NEC motion.'[23]

And when Ian MacGregor took up office on 1 September the battle lines were quickly drawn. One of his first acts as Chairman was to warn the union of what was to come, saying the industry was producing too much coal at too high a cost. When he later made it clear that the Board's final offer on pay that year was 5·2 per cent, relations between the Board and the NUM quickly worsened. A Special NUM Delegate Conference called an overtime ban, starting on the last day of October. The ban was on two issues, again linking the immediate issue of pay with the more important fight over closures.

The overtime ban led to a rash of disputes between the union and pit managers. The problems were most acute in Scotland and Yorkshire. In Scotland, the Board announced the closure of Polmaise, near Stirling; this was followed by the announcement of the closure of Bogside Colliery. The Board said this was a direct result of the overtime ban, since the pit had flooded because men refused to carry out safety work at weekends.

The Board claimed that overall the overtime ban was having very little effect on coal stocks and that they could last indefinitely. Miners were losing a lot of money, and in some areas there were signs of opposition to the ban. This possibly showed itself in January, in the election to succeed Lawrence Daly as NUM Secretary. The right-wing candidate, John Walsh, the NUM North Yorkshire agent, who argued for a ballot and who was seen as the 'anti-overtime ban' candidate, lost by only 3,615 votes to Peter Heathfield, the Derbyshire Secretary. The result certainly scared the Left.

On the other hand, an opinion poll showed that most miners were happy to continue with the ban.[24] But when in late February the York-shire Council discussed the idea of escalating the ban to strike action it was decisively rejected by more than three to one.

But Yorkshire was also experiencing a number of minor disputes at individual pits: at Denby Grange, over men transferred from Bullcliffe Wood; at the South Kirkby-Ferrymoor Riddings complex over a new privately run washery; and, the most important, a strike in the whole of the South Yorkshire panel, which had begun at Manvers Main. It became known as the 'snap time' dispute, because the management had tried to change the times of meal-breaks for fourteen men, to ease the effects of the overtime ban.

Then, on 1 March, came Cortonwood, the spark which led to the 1984 strike.

Many in the NUM believe that the Coal Board deliberately tried to provoke a national strike, at its convenience. If so, then Yorkshire, one of the NUM's most militant areas, was the ideal place to do it. A strike, or a fourth ballot defeat, might sink Scargill once and for all. A stoppage in the spring would come at just the wrong time of year for the NUM, with coal stocks still very high and summer ahead. Some people in the NUM therefore believe that the South Yorkshire NCB Director, George Hayes, was told to close Cortonwood by London.

But Jack Taylor disagrees that Hayes got his orders from London: 'I think George Hayes decided for himself, and then told London. His terms of reference are economic. He's got to raise coal at less than £26 a tonne. There are pits he could have taken out with less trouble, but there's a longer-term plan we never see – how they see South Yorkshire in ten years' time. He's got to do it in line with that plan.'[25] According to Hayes: 'I selected Cortonwood because there was no future there, not because it was the most uneconomic pit in the area – it wasn't.'[26]

Hayes made his announcement at the 1 March quarterly review meeting. Three days later, on the Sunday morning, 500 Cortonwood men met at Brampton parish hall – the biggest attendance most people could remember at a branch meeting. 'There was absolute silence,' remembers Jack Wake, the branch secretary. Wake told them that the people who had worked on the Friday afternoon shift could well have seen the last coal mined at Cortonwood. 'I was deliberately dramatic to get everyone's attention.' He told the men that the body of Cortonwood was on the operating table. The area director had got hold of the scalpel and it would seem the body was going to end up in the morgue. 'They were words for the moment. I told them the interests of the older men over fifty were different from the younger men – and the younger men's interests should come first.'[27]

Cortonwood doesn't have a reputation as a militant pit. Wake himself is known as a right-wing Labour councillor, and Cortonwood had been the only branch in South Yorkshire to nominate John Walsh for NUM Secretary. But that Sunday the meeting was angry and the decision was unanimous. They would fight the closure and ask the rest of Yorkshire to take strike action.

Part of the problem at Cortonwood was the resentment from men who had only just been moved from a neighbouring pit, Elsecar, in the previous few months – the last of them only in January. They had been guaranteed a future at Cortonwood: the management had always spoken of another five years' life in the pit. And there was the suddenness of it all – only five weeks before the pit actually ceased production. That meant there would be no time to go through the review procedure normally carried out when a pit closes, although George Hayes insisted he wanted the procedure to go ahead.

The following day, at the Yorkshire Council, the area was called out on strike from the last shift on Friday. It was justified on the area ballot taken more than three years earlier, in which 86 per cent of the Yorkshire area had agreed to strike in the event of a pit closure 'other than on the grounds of exhaustion'.

The time bomb had finally gone off.

On its own, the proposed closure of Cortonwood might not have led to a national strike. But Cortonwood was a good example of what was happening in the industry generally. To break even MacGregor said he needed to close dozens of 'uneconomic' pits such as Cortonwood. On Tuesday 6 March, five days after the Cortonwood announcement, leaders of the three mining unions learnt that the pit was only part of a much larger programme of closures for the immediate future. At a National Consultative Council meeting the Board explained that it was looking for a four million tonne cut in production in 1984–5: the guidance was that twenty pits and 20,000 jobs would have to go.

Six days later, on Monday 12 March, the 1984 strike had begun.

Chapter 7

Pickets and Ballots

We shall not be constitutionalised out of a defence of our jobs.

– Mick McGahey, NUM Vice-President[1]

Every evening the NUM branch officers at Maltby Colliery in South Yorkshire met at the miners' Welfare to plan the following day's picketing. Around seven, one of the officials would arrive back with a brown envelope. Inside would be the instructions for Maltby's pickets. Once they'd read them, the branch officials would get out their road-maps and plan their route for the next morning, taking minor country roads to avoid the police. Similar meetings took place in miners' Welfares, pubs and branch offices all over the Yorkshire coalfield.

The 1984 strike followed the flying-picket strategy of the early 1970s. Only this time the main target was not power stations, docks and coal movements, but almost entirely fellow miners. And this time they had to contend with the biggest police operation ever mounted in this country.

In Yorkshire a central strike control centre was set up in the old Executive Room on the ground floor of the Barnsley NUM headquarters, and manned twenty-four hours a day by members of the Yorkshire Executive. On the walls, alongside the old black-and-white photographs of former miners' leaders, were pinned maps of the Yorkshire and Nottinghamshire coalfields, with red stickers showing all the pits in both areas. On the table in the centre of the room was a bank of five telephones, leaflets, a log-book to record all arrests and other incidents, and, in the corner, a radio which was used to listen to police messages.

The Yorkshire centre was only open on weekdays. Other strike centres, manned seven days a week, were set up for each of the four Yorkshire panel areas – at the Kellingley Social Club for North Yorkshire, Brodsworth Miners' Welfare for Doncaster, the NUM office at Silverwood Colliery for South Yorkshire, and the Junction pub in Barnsley for the Barnsley panel.

Picketing by the Yorkshire area began on the very first day of the strike, Monday 12 March. The Yorkshire NUM Executive had resolved the previous week that 'picketing must be restricted to collieries in the York-shire Area with numbers of pickets limited to no more than 6'.[2]

On 8 March, a week after the Cortonwood announcement, and two days after the NUM leaders had met the Board, the Yorkshire and Scottish areas had gone to the National Executive to ask for official backing for their strikes. The Left wanted to adopt the same strategy they had argued for in 1983, but which then the Executive had turned down. 'I want to make it clear that we are not dealing with niceties here,' explained Mick McGahey. 'Area by area will decide, and in my opinion it will have a domino effect.'[3]

The Executive sanctioned such action and agreed to give support to any other areas which wished to take similar action. The 1984 strike had started. The following day, Arthur Scargill and Peter Heathfield trans-ferred eight and a half million pounds to a bank in the Isle of Man as a precaution against any forthcoming legal action.

Trevor Bell had proposed that the matter should be put to a national ballot under Rule 43 (see Appendix), but although several people spoke in favour of it including Sid Vincent of Lancashire and Henry Richardson from Nottingham, Bell's motion only got three votes – from himself, Roy Ottey of the Power Group, and Ted McKay from North Wales. Even Jack Jones of Leicester and Ken Toon of South Derbyshire voted against.

But the very fact that Bell had proposed the motion at all would prove crucial, as the Right were to find to their cost.

Why had only three Executive members actually voted for a national ballot, when, in seemingly similar circumstances the year before, a majority had rejected Arthur Scargill's plan for a strike under Rule 41, (see Appendix), and insisted on a national ballot?

One reason for the difference may be that in 1983 the South Wales strike had already started and the prospect of disunity within the NUM was already apparent. Executive members were already witnessing con-flicting action between areas, and feeling the pressure for a national ballot. In 1984 no strike was due to start until the following Monday, and Executive members were under less pressure. Had the Executive meeting taken place a week later, or the Cortonwood announcement and NUM meeting with the Coal Board taken place a week earlier, the Executive, facing the likelihood of serious disunity, might have decided differently.

Second, the intervening twelve months had seen the Left achieve a majority on the Executive for the first time in NUM history. In May 1983 the normally right-wing Durham area had elected as its representative a left-wing rank-and-file member, Billy Stobbs. The Left knew they were now in control, and the Right knew they weren't.

But in the first week of the strike thousands of Yorkshire miners poured across county borders into Nottinghamshire, Derbyshire and Lancashire to picket collieries where the men were still working. On some mornings several Nottinghamshire pits had to be closed because of successful mass picketing. When a Yorkshire picket, David Jones, died early on the first Wednesday morning outside Ollerton Colliery, the leaders of both Yorkshire and Nottinghamshire appealed to the pickets to leave. Not all of them did so.

The Nottingham area had agreed to ballot its members on the Friday of the first week. But when the result came through at lunchtime on the Saturday it showed that Notts men had voted three to one to carry on working.

Many NUM members – even within Yorkshire and even many of the pickets themselves – now believe that it was a great mistake for the Yorkshire pickets to rush into Nottinghamshire that first week, before the Notts men had a chance to decide for themselves. The hostility between miners in the two counties goes back a long way, and many people believe that the Nottinghamshire members voted so overwhelmingly against a strike precisely because of the mass picketing. They weren't going to be told by Yorkshire what to do. The same argument applies to Lancashire.

That weekend – 16–18 March – the results of ballots in several other areas were announced. Although there were great variations between areas, all except Northumberland voted against a strike, and this gave the impression that if the NUM had held a national ballot the pro-strike forces would have lost. But, of course, none of the large militant areas had balloted their members, and close examination of the figures showed that in those areas which had balloted there had in fact been a small swing towards strike action since the previous ballot in March 1983. If that trend had been reflected throughout the whole union the necessary 55 per cent vote might well have been attainable. Indeed, a MORI opinion poll for LWT's *Weekend World*, taken on Friday 9 March, showed that 62 per cent of miners were prepared to strike over pit closures, compared with 33 per cent who were not.[4]

After these area ballots the NUM's disunity was all too obvious, and most outsiders assumed that it would only be a matter of time before a national ballot was called. But the next meeting of the Executive, which

would have to call the ballot, wasn't due for almost a month, on Thursday
12 April.

Although only three members of the Executive had actually voted for
a ballot at the March meeting, a ballot now found firm support from others.
Over the next three weeks at least twelve area officials wrote to the NUM
Secretary, Peter Heathfield, asking for the Executive to be reconvened so
that the question of a national ballot could be discussed again. They included (with the dates of their letters given in parentheses) Trevor Bell of
COSA (16 and 27 March), Sid Vincent of Lancashire (17 March), Roy Ottey
of the Power Group (22 March), Henry Richardson of Nottingham, Jim Colgan of the Midlands (16 and 21 March), Ted McKay of North Wales (19
and 26 March), Harry Hanlon of Cumberland, Denis Murphy of Northumberland, Ken Toon of South Derbyshire, Jack Jones of Leicester (21 March),
and Tom Callan of Durham. Ron Dunn of the Durham Mechanics wrote
on 2 April to ask for a ballot but didn't call specifically for a meeting. Most
of the letters had been carefully coordinated by those involved.

Between them they represented thirteen votes on the Executive out of
twenty-four (Nottingham has two NEC seats). In addition, Idwal Morgan
of the Cokemen had written to ask for a Special Conference to be convened.

But an emergency meeting of the Executive never took place. 'A number
of conflicting requests are being received,' Peter Heathfield told Trevor
Bell. 'You may rest assured that the national officials are continuing to
monitor the situation carefully.'[5] 'National officials shall not hesitate to
call a meeting of the NEC should circumstances require it,' he wrote to
Jack Jones.[6] Yet in almost similar circumstances, over Tymawr Lewis
Merthyr Colliery the year before, Arthur Scargill had himself convened an
emergency Executive meeting.

In 1984 the Left seemed to be playing for time. With delay, the other
areas might come out, especially if they were picketed. If a national ballot
eventually had to be held it might be delayed until a point when the Left
were more confident of winning: when men had been on strike for some
time and become used to the hardship, going back to work would mean
their efforts had been wasted.

The Right were totally outmanoeuvred by Arthur Scargill and Peter
Heathfield over the first five weeks of the dispute. The right-wingers of the
Executive were in a minority, and nothing like the force they had been
with Joe Gormley leading them. But a majority consisting of right-wing
Executive members who wanted a ballot, and left-wingers who didn't

want one personally, but had been mandated by their areas to go for one, could have been constructed.

The Right's problem was that it had been some years since they had held regular caucus meetings. In the days when NUM headquarters were in London, Executive members travelled down the day before and stayed overnight, which gave them an excellent opportunity to meet. But after the move to Sheffield most travelled there on the day of the meeting. The only members who didn't were those from distant coalfields (Scotland, South Wales and Kent), who were all on the Left.

Another problem for the Right was that areas they could traditionally count on sometimes chose left-wingers as their NEC representatives, thanks to good organization by the Left. Billy Stobbs in Durham, Jim Colgan of the Midlands, and Henry Richardson from Nottingham were good examples of this.

Furthermore, right-wingers had fallen out with each other after the 1981 Presidential election débâcle. Too many felt that their colleagues were interested only in personal ambition. There was resentment that some of their number seemed to be 'bought off' from time to time by Scargill. On top of that, nobody was prepared to give up the time to organize a right-wing caucus, especially when they no longer had a majority.

Nevertheless, the Right did hold something of a caucus meeting – on 27 March. It was the only one during the whole 1984 dispute.

The idea for the meeting had come from the Secretary of the North Wales miners, Ted McKay. He rang Roy Ottey and suggested that the right-wingers should meet. Ottey agreed with the suggestion and rang Sid Vincent in Lancashire, the man who had traditionally organized such gatherings in the past. Vincent was also keen, and they agreed that the best place to hold the meeting was somewhere in Leicestershire. Ottey then rang the Leicester Secretary, Jack Jones, and asked him to book a hotel room. Together, Ottey and Vincent went through the list of Executive members they felt they could safely ask. Vincent phoned half of them, and Ottey the rest.

Apart from McKay, Jones, Vincent and Ottey, three others had agreed to come: Harry Hanlon from Cumberland, Ken Toon from South Derbyshire and Trevor Bell of COSA. But Ottey couldn't get hold of Ray Chadburn at the Nottingham headquarters – he was in the middle of a court case in London. But the caucus had to have somebody from Nottingham: after all, it was the biggest area and had two Executive members. Ottey didn't know what to do. He couldn't just ring the Nottingham headquarters and ask for somebody else to come. The Notts Secretary, Henry Richardson, a left-winger, might find out what was going on.

Eventually Ottey decided the only option was to ring the Coal Board, where he spoke to Ned Smith, the NCB Industrial Relations Director. 'Ned, I've got to get hold of Ray Chadburn.'

Chadburn rang Ottey a few hours later. He said he couldn't make it but suggested that another Notts full-time official, Roy Lynk, attend in his place, and that he would be able to speak on behalf of the Notts area.

When the eight met at the Brant Inn at Groby, they found reporters and television crews waiting for them. Somebody had spoken to the press. Sid Vincent's initial reaction was to return home at once, but he quickly changed his mind.

With apologies for absence from various other Executive members, the caucus felt they could count on fourteen votes on the Executive – enough for a majority. They agreed to press their case. 'There is now a clear mandate for a national ballot. We are in a majority and the National Executive should reconvene and call a ballot,' proclaimed Jack Jones, the Leicester Secretary.[7]

Their major worry was Jim Colgan, the Executive member for the normally right-wing Midlands area. Colgan had been mandated to vote for a ballot, but earlier in the week of the Executive meeting he had been quoted in the local press as saying he would not do so. He had been arrested a few days earlier on a picket line, and, he alleged, assaulted by the police. This had changed his attitude.

Roy Ottey tried desperately to find Colgan the day before the meeting, but with no luck. He wasn't at his home or at the Midlands office. In the end Ottey didn't see him until a few minutes before the Executive started on the Thursday, at the Sheffield headquarters. (He had spent the whole of the previous day at the NUM headquarters, where nobody had thought of looking for him.) And the Right began to fear that Colgan would vote with the Left.

On the Thursday of the crucial meeting thousands of demonstrators gathered outside the NUM headquarters in Vicar Lane, Sheffield – most of them miners from almost every coalfield, along with the usual Trotskyist newspaper sellers, the Fleet Street industrial correspondents, nearly a dozen television crews and police from eight forces. At one point things had got quite nasty with pickets and police pushing against each other in the square below. Several people were injured and dozens of pickets were arrested.

Inside, battle commenced, but it was all an anti-climax. Had there been a vote it would probably have gone 14–10 or 13–11 in favour of a ballot, but it never came to that. Arthur Scargill simply outmanoeuvred the Right with a move that Joe Gormley would have been proud of.

Scargill reminded the Executive that a motion calling for a national ballot had been discussed at the previous Executive on 8 March and therefore could not be put again at a subsequent meeting: 'I hope you are not going to put me in a position where I have to rule.'

Jack Jones, from Leicester, refused to withdraw his motion and the Executive went through a 'ritual' of discussing a national ballot. But then, after a long debate, Scargill did just what he had said he would do, and simply ruled the motion out of order.

Jones challenged Scargill's ruling and Mick McGahey took the chair. It was then that the carefully constructed pro-ballot coalition crumbled. Since it was now a question of confidence in the chair, several left-wingers felt they were freed from their mandates, which only told them to go for a ballot. Only eight voted against Scargill's ruling – far short of the two-thirds majority required – and the President had won the day.

Scargill proposed that a Special Conference be convened in Sheffield the following Thursday, at which all the motions calling for a ballot could be properly debated. The Conference would also consider a National Executive proposal to change the rules to require only a simple majority in future for strike action under Rule 43, instead of 55 per cent (see Appendix). The leadership had decided that if a ballot was to be held at any point, then it should be made easier to win it, although the idea of changing the rule had been around for a long time.

The NUM delegates gathered in Sheffield City Hall the following week to debate the proposals. Outside, the crowd of striking miners, which included a large contingent from Nottinghamshire, listened to speeches and music while the debates continued inside. The NUM and the police were concerned to keep the crowd entertained so as to avoid the trouble of the previous week.

In the seven days between the Executive and the Conference the separate NUM areas had been deciding how to vote on the two main proposals – a ballot and the rule-change. But Arthur Scargill had little to worry about. Four separate motions calling for a ballot were each rejected – 69–51, 69–55, 70–39 and 100–8. By sixty-nine votes to fifty-four they carried a motion from Kent sanctioning the NEC's calling of a strike under Rule 41 (area by area), and making the Head Office responsible for the future coordination of the strike.

There had been speculation, based on various area decisions, that the rule-change might not go through, but in the end it easily achieved the necessary two-thirds majority.

In the course of five weeks Scargill and the Left had pulled off a brilliant piece of political footwork. They had been able to call a national strike, but without holding a national ballot.

The Left had argued that a ballot was wrong because it would give miners the right to vote other miners out of a job. The arguments were tarnished somewhat by the fact that they had been happy to hold ballots on pit closures in the past. Yorkshire justified its area strike on the 86 per cent vote of 1981, more than three years earlier, but another worry about a ballot for those who supported a strike was put forward by the Yorkshire President, Jack Taylor, at the Special Conference: 'I will tell you what worries me about ballots, and I do not want to be offensive to anybody because we have got enough problems. I will tell you what is up. We don't really trust you. We don't really trust you.'[8]

The 'you' Taylor was referring to was the Nottingham delegation, which had always in recent years produced large majorities against striking. Many in Yorkshire felt that even if a national ballot had been held and it had gone for a strike, there was no guarantee the Notts men would come out. The argument was rather weak – the Notts men did stick to the overtime ban throughout the 1984 dispute.

But after the April Conference the question of a ballot did not come up again for six months (it was next raised at the Executive on 1 November, when only nine voted in favour). The new 50 per cent majority rule was not required. The Left had argued so strenuously that it was wrong to ballot *in principle* (because the subject was pit closures), that it would have been difficult for them to change their minds – it might have looked unprincipled.

The ironic thing is that had the NUM held a national ballot in the first few months of the strike, the Left would almost certainly have won it. Several opinion polls, and experience in the coalfields, would suggest as much. Five separate opinion polls carried out between early March and early July showed that a 55 per cent vote could easily have been achieved. Ironically, the two ITN polls taken after the April Conference, when only a 50 per cent vote was required, both showed that more than 60 per cent of miners were for striking and fewer than 30 per cent against.[9]

After the April Special Conference the Right made no impact either on the Executive or in public. Sid Vincent felt strongly about the pit closures issue and detected a new militancy inside his own area. The hard-line right-wingers knew they could never win on the Executive or in the Conference and decided they would stop opposing the leadership. After April members such as Trevor Bell, who had frequently spoken against Scargill on television, decided to keep quiet since criticism of Scargill would only add to the union's disunity. If the strike was lost, the Right felt, then at least Scargill would get the blame. At Executive meetings, right-wingers said very little and were happy to sit back and hope the Left would argue amongst themselves, as occasionally they did. On one occasion Scargill was being strongly criticized by the South Wales men. 'Good this, isn't it?' said Ottey to his neighbour, Trevor Bell. 'Quiet,' he replied, 'don't let them see you're laughing – just sit back and enjoy it.'

Throughout the summer the miners' strike became a war between striking pickets and working miners, and between striking miners and the police. The police, coordinated from the National Reporting Centre at New Scotland Yard, pumped thousands of men into Nottinghamshire and Yorkshire. Pickets were turned back at the Nottinghamshire border by police road-blocks – and even at the Dartford Tunnel under the Thames on one famous occasion. Thousands of pickets were arrested, creating a long backlog of cases for the courts, while hundreds of police and pickets were injured in picket-line clashes the like of which had not been experienced in living memory.

The Government seems to have prepared well for the strike. Unlike in 1981, it was now ready to confront the miners. The 1972 and 1974 miners' strikes had left deep scars on the Conservative Party and in opposition the Conservatives had worked out what to do to try to ensure they won next time. A Conservative Party report prepared by Nicholas Ridley in 1978 had suggested several measures to be taken on returning to government. Coal stocks should be built up and alternative energy supplies found for the power stations. Social security benefits for strikers' families should be reduced to deter strikes. Employers would be armed with sanctions under the civil law. And the police would work out better national coordination to minimize the effects of flying pickets. Most of the proposals of the Ridley report were carried out during the course of the first Thatcher Government. In 1984 the Government persistently refused to intervene: most of its work had already been carried out.[10]

At the end of May began what was probably the greatest confrontation of the whole dispute. The British Steel coking plant at Orgreave, near Sheffield, was continuing to produce coke for the British Steel works at Scunthorpe, and every day convoys of lorries carried the coke the few miles up the M18. For Arthur Scargill Orgreave became the Saltley of 1984. Only five miles from his office, the site could be reached by Scargill in ten minutes, and he made several appearances – on one occasion being arrested, on another being injured (by a police riot shield he claimed) and had to stay overnight in hospital.

Orgreave involved some nasty scenes, many of which were shown on the nation's television screens. At one point pickets used a telegraph pole as a battering ram, a Portakabin was set alight, and police suffered a hail of stones and bottles. For their part the police were prepared to charge into the crowd on horseback and use their truncheons – one particular incident of a policeman clobbering a picket over the head shocked the nation. But the police organization was too much for the pickets. The police, who came in thousands, bringing men from all over the country, and dressed in riot-gear, overwhelmed the miners. Most days the pickets were simply outnumbered, and police discipline ensured there was never any likelihood of the coke convoy not leaving the plant.

The miners failed at Orgreave because they were disorganized and lacked much of the discipline Scargill had provided at Saltley. The picket had no real leaders. And they lacked the numbers which at Saltley had been provided by the rest of the Birmingham labour movement. The trade union movement was far more demoralized than it had been twelve years previously: in 1984 there was no prospect of Sheffield trade-unionists going on strike to join the Orgreave picket lines.

For the rest of the dispute the mass picketing continued, generally at collieries. Towards the end of the summer the Yorkshire flying pickets had to start picketing their own pits, as other Yorkshire miners began to return to work. The organized and often successful pickets of 1972 and 1974 had turned to token confrontations with the police, which did little except deter others from returning to work, and use up police resources.

As winter approached, neither a ballot nor the pickets had secured the unity the NUM needed to win a strike. Unfortunately for the strikers' cause, the arguments over union democracy and picket-line violence had enabled the Government, the Coal Board and the media largely to ignore the issue behind the dispute – pit closures.

Chapter 8

Land of the Silver Birch

United We Stand, for Unity is Strength
– Motto of the Nottingham Area NUM

In May 1984 a 34-year-old miner from Bevercotes Colliery in Nottinghamshire walked into a branch of a solicitors' office in Ollerton. He was told that they were too busy to help him. 'You'll regret this,' he muttered as he left, and he went instead to the firm's head office at Newark, ten miles away.

There the miner spoke to Andrew Fearn, and told him he was an official of the Nottinghamshire Working Miners' Committee. He wanted legal advice in his campaign against the NUM leadership. Fearn agreed to help. Within a matter of days the Newark office of Hodgkinson and Tallents had virtually become an unofficial anti-strike centre for the working miners and their allies in other coalfields.

The following months were to prove a busy time for Hodgkinson and Tallents, as Fearn and a senior colleague, David Payne, got more and more involved in every detail of the miners' dispute. Before long they probably knew more about the dispute than anybody outside the leadership of the NUM or the NCB.

The miner's name was Chris Butcher. But he would become better known as 'Silver Birch'.

One Thursday morning in late July, Fearn acquired two new important clients, Robert Taylor and Ken Foulstone, two miners from Manton Colliery near Worksop. Geographically, Manton is in Nottinghamshire, but, as far as the Coal Board and the NUM are concerned, it actually belongs to the Yorkshire area. Fearn had been recommended to the two miners by Chris Butcher but Butcher hadn't told Fearn about them. Fearn recalls: 'My secretary had just put in my diary "Thursday 10 am – Robert Taylor and Ken Foulstone". All I had been told was that they were Yorkshire miners – they might have been strikers with charges against them for all I knew.'[1]

But within minutes of their arrival in his office Fearn began to believe the case would have an important bearing on the future of the strike. Taylor and Foulstone had been on strike at Manton since March, and wanted to challenge the Yorkshire and national NUM over the constitutional validity of the strike within the union rules. If their case were successful it could lead to the NUM having to call a national ballot, which they might well lose. Earlier in the dispute Taylor had received considerable publicity when he had tried to get men at Manton back to work, but had no success. His colleague Ken Foulstone could boast of a great-grandfather who had helped sink the original shaft at Cortonwood.

Fearn and Payne spent the whole of that Thursday preparing the case. Early that afternoon they drove with Taylor and Foulstone up the A1 to Retford. There, over lunch in the Happy Eater restaurant, they met the man they came to call 'our mole'. This contact of Taylor and Foulstone from Barnsley furnished the two solicitors with important internal NUM documents obtained from inside the Yorkshire area and NUM national headquarters, and the full verbatim proceedings of all recent NUM Conferences.

Twelve days after Taylor and Foulstone first called at the Newark office, David Payne took them down to London for an appearance at the High Court. Payne knew that once the story broke it would be big news, and that simply for Taylor and Foulstone's own protection he would have to handle the press publicity himself. It so happened that another partner in Hodgkinson and Tallents was Chairman of the Grantham Conservative Association, whose MP is Douglas Hogg, the husband of Sarah Hogg, Economics Editor of *The Times*. Payne rang Sarah Hogg for advice on how to handle the media coverage. She naturally told him to inform *The Times* first of any developments, and to send press releases round to the rest of Fleet Street. Hogg also gave Payne the home phone number of Sir Alastair Burnet, the ITN newscaster.

For the next two days Payne toured London newspaper offices and radio and television studios, handing out press releases and arranging interviews with his two clients. But of all the publicity the Yorkshire miners' case received, an article in the *Daily Express* proved to be the most useful.[2]

Until now nobody had really worked out where the money would be found to pay for the Taylor–Foulstone case. Chris Butcher had offered some of the funds he'd been able to raise, but it would by no means cover the costs of a full-scale legal action in the High Court. 'The *Express* came and asked us who was paying for all this. Well, quite frankly, we were flying blind as far as costs were concerned,' Fearn recalls. 'So they offered to publish a PO Box Number where members of the public could send money to. So straight away we opened the "Miners Ballot Fund" at PO Box 20, Newark, and it appeared at the bottom of an article in the *Express*.'[3]

Within a week the fund had raised £10,000, and within a month, £34,000. That flow of funds provided further publicity in the papers and on television. Donations arrived from members of the public all over the country. Generally it was five or ten pounds at a time, but some small companies sent large sums. One bank manager in the West Country wrote to say he was resigning from his union, ASTMS, in protest at their attitude to the strike, and sent £18, the equivalent of his ASTMS subscription for the next six months.

The Hodgkinson and Tallents premises in Newark were already a press office for Taylor and Foulstone; television and newspaper interviews were held there. Now it became a contact point for anyone who wanted to assist the working miners' campaign against the strike.

Payne and Fearn were occupied almost full-time on the miners' strike, working most evenings and weekends as well. Fearn even had to give up playing cricket every Sunday for the local Newark team. 'It just wasn't the sort of case you could leave at five-thirty and stop thinking about when you went home.'[4]

As well as acquiring every document which might conceivably be relevant to the case against the NUM, the two solicitors scoured the local and national press every morning for the latest developments. Previously the office had taken only *The Times*; now they bought every paper. A scrapbook was compiled of all the relevant cuttings and they built up a contact list of journalists' work and home telephone numbers to keep the media in touch with their latest moves.

For Taylor and Foulstone's High Court action in late September Payne spent sixty-two hours setting out their affidavit, which relied heavily on quotations from internal NUM documents. One afternoon Fearn booked a room in a hotel just north of Newark, and miners from Yorkshire came, one by one, to make sworn statements of how their own branches had been conducting affairs since the strike began. Finally, when the case was ready, Payne drove down to Brighton, where NUM leaders were at the TUC Conference. He waited on the terrace of the Grand Hotel, armed with a photograph of Peter Heathfield. When he spotted him, the writ was served.

The miners of Nottinghamshire have always been different from those of other British coalfields – more 'moderate' or 'right-wing'. Geographically, Yorkshire and Nottinghamshire may have a common border, and many of their mines are only a few miles apart, but in terms of industrial politics they are very different.

Nottinghamshire miners earn some of the biggest bonuses in the country, and relatively few of the coalfield's pits are threatened with closure in the near future. The greater profitability of the Notts coalfield has long been a source of division with other areas. This was illustrated as long ago as the miners' lock-out of 1893, when the British coal owners wanted their men to take a cut in wages, to reflect a recent drop in the price of coal. But the Nottinghamshire coal companies found they could still easily make a profit at the existing wage rates, and half-way through the dispute caused a split among the coal owners by taking their men back to work on the old rates. That move in Nottinghamshire was eventually to lead the miners to victory nationally. After 1893 several Nottinghamshire coal companies formed their own owners' association and granted their workers the first five-day week in the industry. Over the years the Nottinghamshire coalfield saw the development of a special, more cooperative, even collaborative, relationship between the owners and the men. That relationship survives to this day.

But it was the famous 1926 lock-out which really brought out the differences between Nottinghamshire and other areas. At two new Notts pits, Clipstone and Blidworth, where they had only recently started to dig coal, the men continued to work throughout most of the dispute (in doing so they had the approval of some of the Nottinghamshire Miners' Association (NMA) officials – on the grounds that they were doing 'development work'). These two collieries proved to be the thin end of the wedge. By the end of August 1926, four months after the dispute began, thousands of Notts men had drifted back. The situation in Nottinghamshire in 1926 has remarkable parallels with the events of 1984.

According to the General Secretary of the Nottinghamshire Miners' Association in 1926: 'some three or four of the collieries had imported police, and charges are being made of a wholesale character; men brought to the courts on the most trivial offences; there is almost a state of terror in these particular districts'.[5]

Just as Arthur Scargill made frequent visits to Nottinghamshire at the start of the 1984 strike to get the men out, so in 1926 the miners' leader A. J. Cook, Scargill's hero, addressed many mass meetings in the county. For a while Cook's great oratory had some effect, and after Cook's visits in 1926 some men did resume the strike, at least for a day or two.

Then, as now, the position of the officials of the Nottinghamshire Miners' Association was a difficult one. At first they were firm in their support for the strike and tried desperately to prevent men going back. But, as more miners returned to work, branches at some collieries asked their officials to negotiate local settlements with the owners. When the Nottinghamshire President, George Spencer, agreed to meet with one such branch, he was promptly expelled from the Miners' Federation conference.

By early November, Spencer felt forced to side with his own Nottingham men. Until then the back-to-work movement had been proceeding without any encouragement or cooperation from Spencer. It is often believed that Spencer himself masterminded the return to work, but this is wrong. It was only when Spencer realized that the movement was unstoppable that he assumed its leadership. Aware that his own career as a politician (he was a Labour MP with ambitions of higher office) and as a trade-unionist was in ruins, Spencer felt he had no other option. He feared his miners might be exploited if they returned to work without the protection of a union. In many cases settlements were negotiated which involved only a small increase in hours, a small reduction in wages, and much better terms than the other coalfields were eventually forced to accept. Ostracized by the rest of the miners' union, Spencer quickly concluded he had no option but to form a breakaway union in Nottinghamshire, and to secure recognition from the coal owners.

By the end of November 1926 most of the other coalfields had returned to work. After more than six months on strike the miners had been defeated by hardship and hunger. They were forced to accept reduced wages and increased hours. Among the very last to go back were the Nottinghamshire miners' neighbours from Yorkshire.

The Nottinghamshire Miners Industrial Union (NMIU), as the Spencer union was officially called, survived for eleven years – mostly in Nottinghamshire, but with some support in other areas, notably South Wales.

It was despised by miners elsewhere and the rest of the labour movement. It became known as the 'gaffers'' union and described itself as 'non-political'. Spencer received tremendous cooperation from the coal owners, on the understanding that the union would 'eliminate strikes'.[6] The idea of conflict between 'us and them' was replaced by a relationship between 'masters and men'. 'Communists and agitators' were excluded from membership, not that they would have wanted to join anyway. There is also evidence that Spencer received funds from Conservative politicians.

At many Notts pits, subscriptions to Spencer's union were automatically deducted from the men's wages. At some collieries the management put considerable pressure on the men to join the new union when they went back in 1926. George Jelley from Mansfield, now retired, recalls that, when he returned to work at Welbeck in 1926, he was told he could only have a job if he joined the Spencer union. At first he stood by his principles, and refused to take work on such conditions, but a few days later hardship forced Jelley to return to Welbeck – and join the Spencer union.[7]

But in spite of management assistance only a minority of Notts miners were members of Spencer's union. The old union, the Nottinghamshire Miners' Association, survived, albeit weak and unrecognized, and with few members. But whereas before 1926 most Notts miners belonged to the Association, the important thing now was that a majority of Notts miners didn't belong to any union.

Spencerism and non-unionism was particularly strong in the mines of North Nottinghamshire, opened early this century in the area north-east of Mansfield known as the Dukeries.

The wealthy aristocrats who owned this land decided to mine the coal beneath it late in the day. Because the seams were so deep down, extracting it required heavy investment for it to be reached. So they brought in outside companies to dig the coal and recruit the labour. Today, the mines of the Dukeries coalfield are some of the richest in Britain and would be prime targets should any government want to privatize parts of the coal industry.

When these mines were opened in the 1920s their new professional owners developed a special paternalistic relationship with the people they employed. The companies went to great lengths to acquire the necessary labour to ensure that their large capital investment was worth while. With little population in the immediate vicinity, miners had to be attracted from other areas, such as Scotland, South Wales and the North East. The companies built new model villages, such as Welbeck, Harworth and New Ollerton. The miners' houses – a lot better than anything miners lived in elsewhere – were relatively spacious and had gardens. The estates were well laid out and in Ollerton each dwelling was provided with running hot water from the local pit.[8]

The coal companies of the Dukeries effectively controlled the villages they built, with little interference or assistance from outside. They had by-laws regulating the estates where their workers lived: in some instances pet animals were prohibited, and people could be fined 2/- for walking on their own front lawns. The companies even employed their own policemen. To foster a good community spirit they paid for the building of miners' welfare institutes and started local cricket and football teams. In Ollerton the Butterley Company paid for the building of an Anglican church right in the centre of the village – in spite of the fact that the Butterley family were themselves Quakers. The church of St Paulinus was originally intended as 'a cathedral for the new coalfield', and Sir Giles Gilbert Scott, architect of Liverpool's Anglican cathedral, was originally paid to design it, although his plans were later rejected.

But while the men were looked after if they behaved, if they stepped out of line they could expect to be sacked, and any miner who lost his job at the pit automatically lost his home too. After 1926, many miners who had been active in the old union consequently lost their jobs.

As might be expected, left-wing politics was not encouraged: such was the grip the coal company had that it would simply have been impossible to book a room anywhere in the village to hold a left-wing meeting. No Labour Party branch was set up in the new villages until the Second World War. The result was that nearly all local councillors were Conservatives or independents.

The arguments between the Spencer union and the traditional Nottinghamshire Miners' Association came to a head in 1936 and 1937 at Harworth, at the very northern tip of Nottinghamshire, only a few hundred yards from the Yorkshire border and well away from the rest of the Nottinghamshire coalfield. By 1936 the Spencer union had become weak at Harworth and its members outnumbered by miners belonging to the old union. A number of NMA men at the colliery struck over dirt allowances, but at the heart of the dispute was the management's refusal to recognize the Nottinghamshire Miners' Association. So bitter were the feelings aroused by the strike that hundreds of police were brought in to protect those miners who carried on working – as every day the 'chain gang' walked down the street to the pit, watched on either side by the striking miners and their families. On one occasion miners accompanying a hearse proceeding down the main street to a funeral suddenly abandoned the cortège to attack a group of working miners they met *en route.*

Those who remember 1937 say the violence in Harworth then was much worse than in 1984, even though the village saw some of the worst incidents of the 1984 strike.

Harworth achieved national prominence, becoming the Grunwick or Warrington of its day. The left-wing Labour MP and barrister Sir Stafford Cripps came north to defend miners who had been arrested, offering his services free of charge. When, one April evening, a riot broke out in the village, and cars were overturned and shop windows smashed, Harworth made the front-page headlines in London. The Prime Minister, Stanley Baldwin, felt obliged to intervene and, as a result, within a few weeks an amalgamation was arranged between the two Nottinghamshire unions with Spencer becoming President of the new amalgamated union.

The memory of Spencerism lives on today. On the Nottinghamshire picket lines throughout the 1984 strike young miners from Yorkshire often referred to the Spencer union, although in many cases not even their fathers were alive in 1926. In the mining villages of Nottinghamshire some still remember whose grandfathers or fathers were in which union, and grudges are still borne.

The right-wing nature of the Nottinghamshire coalfield persisted throughout the post-war period, with the men generally earning better wages than could be expected elsewhere. Thousands of men were brought into this expanding coalfield from Scotland and the North East as pits closed in these areas in the 1950s and 1960s. One large housing estate in Welbeck village is known as the 'Geordie estate' and in certain parts of the county a Geordie accent is as familiar as a Nottinghamshire one.

While the movement of Scots, Welsh and North East miners to Yorkshire is thought to have aided the radicalization of that once right-wing coalfield, immigrant miners in Nottinghamshire who might once have been militant on the whole seem to have adopted the more conciliatory nature of the Notts men: persuaded perhaps by the higher levels of pay, and, at most pits, by the prospect of a more secure future.

Frequently Nottinghamshire, now the second-largest coalfield, has led the right-wing opposition to the NUM Left. In the 1969 unofficial strike pickets came down from Yorkshire to try to get the Notts men out. In 1972 and 1974 the coalfield was fully behind the strike but in the late 1970s Notts was among the areas which led the moves towards an incentive scheme, and it was among the first coalfields to negotiate such a scheme at an area level.

Politically, it is argued that Nottinghamshire has seen the emergence of the Tory miner. In April 1977 the supposedly safe Labour mining seat of Ashfield unexpectedly returned a Tory MP in a by-election – overturning a Labour majority of nearly 23,000. It was the most surprising by-election defeat for Labour of the 1974–9 Parliament, and some commentators believed that one of the reasons for the massive swing was that the highly paid Ashfield miners were voicing their displeasure at the Labour Government's Social Contract which was denying them even higher wages.

Ashfield returned to the Labour fold in 1979. More worrying for Labour though was the 1983 Conservative victory in the new constituency of Sherwood, whose boundaries contain ten collieries and one of the highest concentrations of miners in any seat in Britain. Even Mansfield, with a Labour majority of only 2,216, must technically be considered a 'marginal' now. The 1984 strike will probably have worsened the Labour Party's problems. More than five thousand miners asked to stop paying the political levy. The new MP for Sherwood, Andrew Stewart, joked that he might become the first NUM-sponsored Tory MP!

The leadership of the Notts area is divided between a right-wing President, Ray Chadburn, and a left-wing General Secretary, Henry Richardson. At first, in 1984, Chadburn and Richardson regarded themselves as the servants of their members and pressed the National Executive to hold a national ballot, as the Notts men clearly wanted. Life was extremely difficult for the two officials, who came under increasing attack from both sides. After the Executive meeting in Sheffield on 12 April Chadburn and Richardson were physically attacked by pickets waiting outside; they were jostled, kicked, punched and verbally abused. Some of the pickets were annoyed that the two men were calling for a ballot, and, thanks to a somewhat misleading impression created by media coverage of events, the protesters probably believed, mistakenly, that the two officials were opposed to the strike itself. Very angry with the media, Chadburn turned on an ITN crew and tried to stop the cameraman filming what was going on, while Richardson tried to calm him down.

During the hour-long drive in Chadburn s car back to Mansfield they decided they'd had enough. Why should they continue to suffer physical and verbal abuse for a principle they didn't even believe in. On arriving back at the Notts area headquarters they found another camera crew waiting for their reaction to the violence against them in Sheffield. Richardson told the waiting journalists he now wanted all Notts men to join the strike.

Indeed, in the early weeks, more and more Nottinghamshire men did seem to be joining the strike, or at least staying away from work. The position was often misreported by journalists who frequently gave the impression that all Nottinghamshire mines were at work as normal. Night after night television and radio bulletins said that all mines in Nottinghamshire were 'working normally', when in reality all had at least some men on strike. At Welbeck, for instance, half the work-force were out at one point. And throughout the 1984 strike Nottinghamshire men continued to observe the overtime ban begun in October 1983, and suggestions that they might accept the 5.2 per cent pay offer were quickly rejected.

But those miners who carried on working grew increasingly antagonistic to the Notts area leadership, who they felt were not adequately representing or protecting their interests.

Several of those NUM branch officials who were still working kept in regular contact with each other informally, phoning each other regularly to say how many men were working at their pits and so on, but, with the Notts Area NUM then in the control of strikers, the working miners, although a majority, were disorganized and isolated.

One morning in April, Chris Butcher, disheartened and angry about the intimidation faced by working miners, decided to do something about it.

'All I'd ever organized before were leaving parties for blokes at work who were retiring,' he says. By that afternoon Butcher had arranged a meeting with representatives of working miners from virtually every pit in North Nottinghamshire.

A few days later Butcher attended a working miners' rally outside the Notts area headquarters in Mansfield. Seven thousand working miners came to make their feelings known as an important Area Council meeting was going on. Meanwhile, striking miners occupied the building. Both sides confronted each other, separated by police. It was an impressive show of force by the working miners. It had been organized not by Butcher but by two branch officials from Bentinck Colliery who were themselves in favour of the strike but felt a duty to represent the feelings of the men they were elected to represent. Butcher went round the demonstration handing out slips of paper with his name and telephone number, and asked miners who wanted to form a pro-work organization to contact him.

The result was the Nottinghamshire Working Miners' Committee. The committee – effectively a gathering of representatives from all the Nottinghamshire pits – elected ten officials, including a Chairman, Vice-Chairman, Treasurer and Secretary. It set out its aims as:

1. To form a link-up of all 25 Notts pits to stop rumours spreading throughout the Notts coalfield.

2. To assist miners who are still working for the sake of democracy and may be being intimidated.

3. To do all in its power to re-affirm democracy within the NUM *and not to break or replace it* [their emphasis].[9]

The committee distributed leaflets to working miners informing them how they should tell the police of any intimidation, and they drew up forms for miners to claim compensation from the Coal Board for any loss they incurred through intimidation. They raised their own funds, and in cases where the NCB wouldn't pay compensation the committee would itself pay. One working miner was bought a new bicycle; another was given four days' pay to make up for the time he had off work after being beaten up.

But the problem for the working miners in Nottinghamshire was that although they undoubtedly constituted a majority among the union membership, most NUM branch officials and members of the Nottinghamshire Area Council and Executive were solidly in favour of the strike and weren't at work. In June came an opportunity for working miners to change things. In branch elections throughout the coalfield dozens of pro-strike officials were swept from office and replaced by men still at work. Although the Notts men on strike claimed that many of their supporters had been unable to vote, the trend in favour of the men at work was unmistakable. Twenty-seven of the thirty-one delegates to the Notts Area Council were now working miners along with every single member of the Notts Area Executive – apart from Ray Chadburn and Henry Richardson.

After the June elections the Working Miners' Committee met less frequently. Many Nottinghamshire miners felt that now they had control of their area there was no need for a separate organization.

Chris Butcher meanwhile had new plans. He had been contacted by Jim Lord, the secretary of Agecroft Colliery in Lancashire, who was likewise still working. Butcher had invited Lord to a meeting of the Notts Working Miners' Committee and in turn Lord invited Butcher and some colleagues back to Lancashire, where Butcher addressed a meeting of 300 working miners in the canteen at Agecroft. Afterwards, while Butcher was chatting to some of the Agecroft men, it was suggested by one miner that Butcher's nickname ought to be 'Silver Birch'. because of the grey streaks in his hair and because he had the sturdiness of a tree. Butcher says he didn't take much notice of the comment at the time.

After his trip to Lancashire Butcher decided it would be a good idea to visit other areas where men were still working and meet some of the people who had already rung him at home. For two weeks – his official holiday – Butcher toured the country, accompanied by the Industrial Editor of the *Mail on Sunday*, Chris Leake. Travelling 4,000 miles in all, he visited working miners in South Wales, Staffordshire, North Wales, Warwickshire, Lancashire again and Scotland.

On one occasion in South Wales, Butcher got into a telephone conversation with a journalist in London. He explained to the reporter that he was going round visiting miners who were at work or who wanted to work. 'What's your name?' the journalist inquired. 'I'd prefer to keep that secret at this stage,' Butcher replied, and then, suddenly remembering the conversation in Lancashire a few days earlier, 'just call me Silver Birch.'

'The next day in Staffordshire', Butcher recalls, 'I was absolutely amazed when I saw all the "Silver Birch" headlines on the front pages.'[10]

The Silver Birch story, coming as it did in the middle of Fleet Street's 'silly season', aroused considerable press interest. The story was tied in with the press's increasing speculation, fuelled by the Coal Board, about a drift back to work. And the mystery surrounding Silver Birch's anonymity only increased the speculation. Miners who knew Silver

Birch's identity were offered more than a thousand pounds to reveal it. They all refused. Chris Leake, meanwhile, had run a *Mail on Sunday* 'exclusive' of his week spent with Silver Birch. Leake said it was the cheapest 'exclusive' the paper had ever produced.

The NUM quickly nicknamed Silver Birch 'Dutch Elm', and some union officials questioned whether he really existed, suggesting that he was actually several different people doing the same thing. Amid the speculation several other Notts miners were accused of being Silver Birch.

The following Sunday, Butcher allowed Leake to reveal his identity and the press descended on Butcher's council house in Ollerton. For a while the press attention became too much for him, and after one press conference on his front lawn Butcher burst into tears and rushed inside.

But amid all the media attention Butcher felt his campaign had begun to bear some fruit. Anti-strike miners in the areas and pits he had visited now had more confidence, he argued. Some began to form their own working miners' committees. To assist them Butcher handed out copies of the forms he had used for his own committee in Nottinghamshire.

Butcher held several national meetings with miners from all over the country, which often took place at the Green Dragon pub in Mansfield. The gatherings were well attended – with more than a hundred people on some occasions. Some of the miners who came were working miners while others were still on strike, if unwillingly. Butcher often paid the petrol expenses of the men still striking, and provided those present with a meal and several pints of beer. It was all paid for from the thousands of pounds Butcher had received during the course of his campaign. The meetings were mainly an opportunity for the anti-strike miners to air their views and to learn from each other. In an alcove at the back of the room often sat the two Newark solicitors David Payne and Andrew Fearn taking notes and gathering evidence for their legal cases. But for several months Butcher's efforts had little result. Until November, only a handful of miners had returned to work in each area, although the Coal Board made great publicity over a 'drift back to work', and during the August 'silly season' its importance was exaggerated by the media.

Butcher's campaign was a highly personal one. His finances were termed the 'Chris Butcher Fund for Democracy', and the exercise book he carried containing his contacts' names and addresses was called the 'Book of Friendship'. The publicity and mystery over 'Silver Birch' put off some potential supporters, and, at times, Butcher seemed to see himself as the saviour of the working miners.

Chris Butcher soon fell out with his colleagues on the Notts Working Miners' Committee, who disliked his campaign. 'You've made yourself into a film star,' Butcher was told. They suggested privately that he was in danger of breaching the NUM rules. Colin Clarke and John Liptrott, the first Notts miners to take the NUM to court, soon got together with men from other areas and set up their own National Working Miners' Committee, which elected officers and drew up a constitution. The national committee was mainly confined to Nottinghamshire and Staffordshire, but claimed to link the several area working miners' committees established around the country. Its members were mostly right-wing labour NUM branch officials, concerned about the way the NUM was being run. Most of Butcher's contacts, on the other hand, were ordinary miners concerned about getting back to work.

The National Working Miners' Committee also based its operations at a solicitor's office, Ellis Fermor in Ripley, where David Negus got just as involved in the dispute as Fearn and Payne in Newark were. By the end of October they had raised more than a hundred thousand pounds, though £30,000 of this was spent on a full-page advertisement in *The Times* and two half page ads in the *Daily Mail* and *Daily Express*. (These sums were insignificant, however, compared with the several millions raised by striking miners and their supporters in the labour movement and elsewhere.) Critics alleged that much of the money came from private business, but the committee insisted that most of the donations were from private individuals. The committee spent most of its efforts funding and supporting various legal actions, and publicizing the working miners' case. For instance, they held fringe meetings at the Liberal and SDP conferences.

The National Working Miners' Committee and Butcher's group were largely carrying out the same kind of activities. Butcher, Clarke and Liptrott were all founder members of the Nottinghamshire Working Miners' Committee, but there were serious personal differences between the two groups. Clarke and Liptrott disliked the personal nature of Butcher's work; Butcher thought they were ineffective. Both sides accused each other of not using their money properly, of damaging the NUM and of having links with business and the Conservative Party. At times relations grew quite bitter.

The NUM leadership and various journalists tried to establish links between the working miners' groups and the Conservative Party, the Coal Board and right-wing pressure groups. It was said that the working miners were funded by people with right-wing connections. Donations by Lord Taylor of Taylor Woodrow and Hector Laing of United Biscuits, both contributors to Conservative Party funds, were quoted as examples. But such accusations were not totally fair to the working miners. Donations from people who contribute to the Conservative Party are no more relevant than the fact that Libya might fund the IRA. When an organizer from the right-wing Freedom Association toured the coalfields to offer his services, he met with a frosty response.

More significant perhaps were the links between the National Working Miners' Committee and David Hart, a flamboyant businessman, and former bankrupt, who acts as a part-time adviser to Mrs Thatcher. These were first exposed by Paul Foot in the *Daily Mirror*.[11] In the early days of the committee David Hart seemed to be playing a leading role, and one of the committee's first meetings was held at Hambledon Hall, an expensive hotel in Leicestershire owned by Hart's brother. Another meeting was scheduled to take place at Claridges, where Hart has a suite.

The Working Miners' Committee's first secretary, Bob Copping, who is also secretary of the Barnsley Winders, resigned in protest at Hart's influence on the committee and because he thought it was becoming an 'anti-trade union organization'.[12] He was very unhappy about Hart's links with the Government and the Coal Board. Copping says that Hart was presented to him as the 'money man', and claims that at one meeting somebody came in to the room and told Hart that 'Number Ten' was on the phone. Hart himself admits that he did give the committee a hundred pounds, but argues that he went to committee meetings purely as a journalist. He says that the meetings were sometimes held at locations arranged by him, simply to make it easier for him to meet the committee in his role as a journalist. In justification, Hart points to an article he wrote for *The Times* in September about the working miners.[13]

According to Copping the Hambledon Hall meeting was held on Saturday 25 August, with David Hart present. Only three days earlier, on Wednesday 22 August, Hart had spent several hours with Ian MacGregor, advising the Coal Board Chairman about his debate with Arthur Scargill on Channel 4 News that evening. Hart was even in the room while MacGregor was appearing on air, and at one point passed him a piece of paper advising MacGregor of a particular telling point to make against Scargill. That evening Hart and MacGregor had dinner together.

And Bob Copping was not the only man to resign because of David Hart's influence with Ian MacGregor. When the Coal Board's long-standing Head of Public Relations, Geoffrey Kirk, decided to take early retirement in November, after a row with MacGregor, Hart's unofficial role was cited as one of his reasons for going.

The National Working Miners' Committee must have known Hart's connections, simply because, according to Copping, Hart actually boasted about them at committee meetings. However, it seems that after September David Hart stopped attending the working miners' meetings, since several people who joined the committee later say that they never met him.

Most of the leaders of the working miners were in fact right-wing Labour Party supporters, who opposed the way Arthur Scargill was running the union. For example, Tony Morris, the Press Officer of the Working Miners' Committee, was a veteran of Saltley and had in fact voted to strike when the Midlands area voted in March. Morris says he only returned to work because he saw he was in a minority in his area, and in protest at the fact that there was no national ballot.

When Margaret Thatcher sent a letter to working miners in Nottinghamshire thanking them for staying at work, there were wide protests. Many of the working miners resented the assumption that they supported the Coal Board's position, and many insisted that they were only continuing at work in protest that there had been no ballot.

The refusal by the working miners to go on strike, and the campaign carried out by the working miners' organizations, undoubtedly aided the Coal Board and the Government in their battle against the NUM. But the differences between the working miners and striking miners in 1984 were also another reflection of the growing differences within the labour movement in general over recent years.

At the end of September the legal action taken by Robert Taylor and Ken Foulstone came up in the High Court. The NUM chose not to appear at the hearing and Mr Justice Nicholls found in favour of the two Yorkshire miners, ruling that both the Yorkshire and national strikes were 'unofficial' and 'unlawful'. That night Arthur Scargill defied the decision on ITN's Channel 4 News: 'The High Court decision, as far as we are concerned, will not be accepted.'[14]

The following Monday, while sitting in the hall at the Labour Party Conference in Blackpool, Arthur Scargill was served with a court order alleging contempt of court – the man who served it had got through conference security by bribing a steward. The NUM was fined £200,000 for contempt, and Arthur Scargill £1,000. When the union refused to pay, the court tried to sequestrate its assets, but with little success, since much of the NUM's money had been sent abroad. Arthur Scargill's fine was paid, probably against his wishes, by an anonymous donor.

The working miners' guerrilla war against the NUM leadership was totally unprecedented in a major industrial dispute. It is ironic that when the Government and the Coal Board were reluctant to use the Government's trade union legislation against the NUM (legislation which had been designed specifically to deal with such disputes), members of the union itself should have been so willing to go to court – and under old, long-established legislation such as the law of contract, not the Prior or Tebbit laws.

Both the national anti-strike groups stressed that they weren't trying to establish a rival organization to the NUM, but some working miners admit that events might force that situation to come about.

In July an NUM Special Conference introduced a new rule (which had been under discussion before the strike) whereby miners could be disciplined by their areas or the national union 'any omission which may be detrimental to the interests of the union'. The committees proposed to carry out the action were quickly dubbed 'Star Chambers' by the press. But the Conference decision was invalidated by Mr Justice Megarry in the High Court even before the Conference itself had begun. Seventeen Nottinghamshire miners argued that it would be unconstitutional because the Nottingham Area Council had been unable to mandate their Conference delegation since striking miners had occupied the area headquarters on the day the meeting was due to take place. At another Special Conference, a few weeks later, the rule-change was passed again, only to be declared unlawful again by the High Court. But the NUM still went ahead and set up the disciplinary committees.

When the strike is over, men like Butcher, Clarke and Liptrott will become obvious targets for such disciplinary action. Relations during the strike have become so bitter that afterwards there are bound to be attempts at reprisals – by both sides. It is not difficult to see how Spencerism could return to the mining industry.

Chapter 9

A Question of Leadership

It is only by politicising our membership that we will ever bring about the irreversible shift towards a socialist system in society.

– Arthur Scargill, April 1981[1]

Few political figures in this country arouse such strong feelings as Arthur Scargill. 'A vaudeville socialist – he likes nothing better than coming out of the make-up room,' is the description given of him by one senior member of the Labour Party with strong mining connections. Those who dislike Scargill often positively detest him. And yet among his own supporters he is almost worshipped. To the young men on the miners' picket lines he is like a pop-star. They have a trust in him, and a respect for him, that no other British trade union leader or politician in living memory has enjoyed.

Rank-and-file activists in the labour movement share that adulation. The 1984 Labour Party and TUC conferences showed that beyond doubt; yet many labour leaders, on the TUC General Council and in the Shadow Cabinet, dislike and distrust him. Many TUC figures would agree with Neil Kinnock's assessment that Scargill is the 'labour movement's nearest equivalent to a First World War general' [2]

But, whatever his popularity, Scargill is one of the most able leaders a trade union has ever had: a man of outstanding qualities.

He is one of the best public speakers in modern political life, able to speak at length and off the cuff, and to rouse an audience.

His work in the NUM has shown him to be a first-class administrator, able to get to grips with subjects quickly, and possessing an excellent memory for detail. Just after the start of the 1984 dispute Scargill spent several days in the High Court in a case over the miners' pension scheme. The NUM had dismissed its counsel and Scargill himself decided to act for the union in court. He spent several hours on his feet, presenting the NUM's case, cross-examining witnesses, and using all the legal ritual expected of a professional barrister. Although the NUM lost the case, Scargill's advocacy received the highest praise from the judge. And his performance had come at a time when the NUM leader must have had several other things on his mind.

Scargill is highly intelligent. He has managed to overcome the educational disadvantage of having left school at fifteen, and is largely self-taught. He has a sharp mind, reads fast and grasps issues quickly. Few people know as much about the mining industry as he does. But his knowledge and education are generally confined to mining and trade union matters, perhaps at the expense of the broader education associated with many other self-taught socialists – men such as Jimmy Reid, Lawrence Daly and Aneurin Bevan, brought up in the Scottish or Welsh left-wing traditions. Such education is a long-established tradition in most mining communities.

One major fault is that he is sometimes careless or over-optimistic in his use of facts, as has been shown by some of his accounts of the early years of his career. 'He will happily use some piece of information he ought to know is not true,' says one NUM official who has worked with him closely. During the 1984 dispute he was constantly accused by the Coal Board of using false information by the Coal Board. He was wildly optimistic in his predictions in April that the Central Electricity Generating Board had only two months of coal stocks left.

In the view of Vic Allen, who has known him for many years, Scargill is 'essentially a shy person who projects himself as compensation for his shyness'.[3] People who meet him in the flesh for the first time are struck by how much his private character differs from the aggressive Scargill they are used to seeing on their television screens or reading about in the papers. They almost always come away with a far more favourable impression. On a personal level he can be charming, polite, respectful, witty, self-deprecating, even modest. He will discuss everyday matters such as where the best fish and chip shop in London is, mimic some well-known politician or pull your leg about something. Only rarely does the natural, relaxed, shy Arthur Scargill come across to the public though – when he appears on TV-am to tell of his 'magic moments', or when the camera cuts away to see him smiling at a joke at the TUC Conference.

The difference between the two Arthur Scargills can only partly be explained by hostile media presentation. True he has been vilified in the tabloid press – 'Christ, when I look at the *Sun*, the *Daily Mail* and the *Daily Express* I don't like me either,' he once joked.[4] Academic research has shown he is often the subject of hostile questioning by interviewers on radio or television. But when appearing in public Scargill does change, and seems to adopt a more aggressive posture, partly, no doubt, because he knows he has to be careful about what he says.

People who know him well say Scargill finds it difficult to make close friends. It seems that only a handful of people have been really close to him over any length of time. And, being such a strong personality, there are quite a few people he has fallen out with. Those who work with him professionally or politically often remark that, even though they may have worked with him for several years, they never really get to know him.

There is a very puritanical aspect to Scargill – the phenomenal work-rate and long hours, the lack of drinking and the dislike for socializing. Scargill is probably incorruptible. He works hard, and he expects the same high standards of his colleagues: he gets very annoyed by NUM staff who drink in office hours or are poor time-keepers.

Arthur Scargill was once told that he had a lot in common with two other major contemporary political leaders, Margaret Thatcher and Tony Benn. All three are extraordinary people with deeply held convictions. All three are highly disciplined workaholics. And, as part of that self-discipline, all three rarely smoke or drink. Scargill took the comparison as a compliment.

And yet Scargill does enjoy the good things in life. He has had a love of big cars since his days in the Young Communist League: 'I've always liked big cars. As a coal face worker I didn't smoke, I didn't drink, but I had a Jaguar.'[5] He likes to wear good suits, to dress smartly and to look neat. He enjoys good food and wine. He bought his daughter a pony; his family have two Airedales. These may seem odd habits for such a committed, left-wing socialist, yet for Scargill there is nothing inconsistent in this. In Scargill's ideal socialist state all people would be entitled to such a high standard of living. He sees his job as striving for just the same standard of living for his own members.

Scargill has the constitution of an ox. During the 1984 dispute he has shown people just how hard he can work, with little sign of fatigue. It has been possible because he has been keeping up a punishing pace for years. Throughout the strike he has constantly travelled the country (and occasionally abroad), making speeches, taking part in negotiations and doing press and television interviews. His way of working seems to be to take on one thing at a time, devote his whole mind and energies to it until the task is complete and then move on to the next item. Scargill has to work particularly hard because he finds it difficult to delegate matters. For instance, the NUM cannot issue a press statement without his having approved it personally: often he writes them himself. He likes to do all NUM press interviews whenever possible.

Over the years Scargill has built up around him a close team of personal staff. Among these are Nell Myers, who officially acts as the NUM press officer and as Scargill's personal assistant (it is a sign of Scargill's style that the two jobs should be held by the same person). She also sat in on some of the negotiations with the Coal Board in 1984. Myers, who comes from San Francisco, is the daughter of an American dockers' leader. She used to work as a free-lance journalist for the *Morning Star* and was formerly married to the television presenter Trevor Hyett. Another American adviser was Peggy Kahn, a Marxist from the University of California, Berkeley, who left the NUM during the summer of 1984. Scargill met her when she was a research student at Sheffield University, doing a PhD on the 'NUM and industrial militancy in the '70s'. Scargill thought Kahn was 'brilliant' and they found that their political views coincided on many issues. The two worked together on various publications, including a pamphlet on workers' control, and Kahn ended up doing personal research work for Scargill. Jim Parker is officially Scargill's driver, but also acts as his bodyguard and can be seen with him everywhere, even getting a seat on the floor of the Labour Party Conference. Parker was at school with Scargill and worked with him when he was President of the Yorkshire area. They are good friends: they once took judo lessons together and Parker has been on holiday with the Scargills. Parker will not hesitate to give Scargill advice if he thinks he needs it. Another close colleague is Mick Clapham, the NUM Head of Industrial Relations, who was associated with the Yorkshire Left in the early 1960s when he was an NUM branch official. Later, after going to university, Clapham joined Scargill's staff in the Yorkshire Compensation Department, and moved to the national union when Scargill became President. Maurice Jones, the editor of *The Miner*, is another who moved from Barnsley to Sheffield.

In the NUM office, relations between Scargill and some of his staff can get very strained. Peggy Kahn's departure in 1984 happened at very short notice. Although it was said that she had been due anyway to return to America to finish her academic work, in reality she had fallen out with Scargill. The problem is that, in relations with his staff, Scargill rightly sees himself as the boss, and so he expects people to do precisely what he asks them to. Perhaps understandably he gets very annoyed when they don't.

Others say Scargill is a good motivator. 'He has tremendous charm, an ability to make you feel you're the only bloke who can do something for him,' recalls one former colleague, who politically is very critical of him. Many others who have worked for Scargill have nothing but praise for him, and say he shows a genuine concern about their problems. Some months after the move to Sheffield, Scargill rang some of those who had decided to stay in London and leave the NUM to ask how they were getting on. When he found out that a couple of them had not yet found jobs, he phoned contacts at the Coal Board and fixed them up with positions there. One right-wing NEC member, whose wife has been suffering from cancer, says Scargill has always shown great concern for her. And Scargill has a great loyalty to many of his staff, as shown by his support for Maurice Jones in 1977; he expects, and usually gets, the same loyalty from them in return.

Relations between Scargill and the NUM staff probably reached their lowest in January 1983, when the headquarters was still in London. Nineteen staff went on strike one day for three and a half hours. The head office secretary of COSA, the NUM staff union, said: 'the relationship with our employer can only be described as akin to those which existed in the nineteenth century with pit owners'.[6] And the strike was not simply a matter of political hostility by former Gormley appointees – among the leaders of the walk-out was the then Head of Research, Steve Bundred, the left-wing GLC councillor who arranged Gerry Adams's visit to London later that year. Some alleged that the real reason for the unrest in the office was the way that Scargill had cracked down on expenses fiddles, which, according to the NUM caretaker, had made 222 Euston Road 'a paradise for fiddlers' and 'like an open coffer' in Joe Gormley's time.[7] A confidential report by a firm of city auditors had recommended several changes in financial procedure. Scargill also abolished the £50 Christmas bonus. Above all, though, staff were unhappy about the move to Sheffield (taken to make the office nearer the coalfields); they felt they hadn't been consulted properly, and most of them didn't want to go. Only three staff out of thirty-six moved to Sheffield, which enabled Scargill to reappoint virtually a whole new headquarters team and wipe the slate clean, taking on people such as Roger Windsor, the NUM's Chief Executive Officer, who came to national prominence after his trip to Libya for the NUM in October 1984.

It is not only NUM staff who occasionally feel Scargill can be dictatorial though. During the 1984 dispute even left-wingers felt the strike was becoming a one-man show, and that people weren't being told what was going on. For instance, very few Executive members were told about the trip to Libya.

The miners' leader is not a man who forgives easily, as shown when the Yorkshire Left originally wanted Jim Oldham to be their candidate for Yorkshire NUM President. Scargill refused to do interviews for Granada Television, even though the station is often sympathetic to trade union causes, simply because of a programme several years ago in which Scargill feels Granada deliberately confronted him with a hostile audience. Similarly, in 1976 Scargill got the Yorkshire NUM Area Council to bar from office two NUM branch officials who had given evidence against him in a libel action. The Council's decision was overturned in the courts and the Yorkshire NUM ruled to be in contempt of court.

Every time Scargill has stood for election in the NUM he has always received an overwhelming majority. A man of great charisma, he has continued to enjoy tremendous support among many of the men he leads. One only needs to see him when he visits the picket lines or goes on a demonstration to appreciate how much faith his men have in him. When pickets sing 'Arthur Scargill, Arthur Scargill, we'll support you evermore', it verges on worship. It is hard to see David Basnett or Terry Duffy getting such a rapturous reception. And Scargill certainly seems to enjoy the support and fame.

'He does have a bit of an ego problem,' says one colleague from Yorkshire. Scargill's vanity is obvious. He loves publicity, the television appearances and the jokes about 'King Arthur' and 'Camelot'. 'I bet it's not often a prince gets introduced to a king like this,' he joked when he met Prince Charles in 1980.[8] Nevertheless, publicly he condemns the cult of personality. It also worries him that people who have not met him dislike him so much; perhaps it would be just as worrying if people had no feelings at all.

Much of Scargill's success in his career has been due to television. From an early stage he saw television as a way of getting himself and his policies known to thousands of miners. He speaks proudly of how he was appearing regularly on television programmes long before he was President of the Yorkshire miners. Over the years he has come to handle the medium very adeptly, and yet he often appears very nervous before doing an interview. But Ian MacGregor acknowledges that when it comes to television Scargill is a 'professional'.[9]

Scargill also has a flair for making the media work for him. Journalists who knew him early in his career say he had the habit of constantly ringing them up with useful pieces of information. Scargill has good relations with a handful of journalists who he feels he can trust. When he talks to a journalist he likes, he will constantly be feeding him useful titbits and leads to follow up. And he has a journalist's understanding of what makes good news.

When, in June 1984, Scargill made an eleven-minute film for Channel 4 News setting out the NUM's side of the dispute, he showed an immediate awareness of how television works. He adapted to the medium naturally, did all his pieces-to-camera in one 'take' without rehearsal. He also appreciated the importance of good images. At the same time, he understood the time constraints of television; he knew he had only a few seconds for each clip of interview.

In turn Scargill himself is hungry for news. As he is driven to work each day he will be listening to the *Today* programme in the car. Each television bulletin during the miners' dispute was eagerly watched and devoured. His office has a video machine to record those bulletins he can't see live, and during the day he will constantly be turning his TV set to the news pages of the teletext services, Ceefax and Oracle. He won't hesitate to ring them up if he thinks they've got something wrong!

It is perhaps ironic for a man who owes much of his success to the media that he should also be one of its greatest critics. For many years now the miners' leader has been attacking what he calls the 'hyenas' and 'filth' of Fleet Street, and the BBC and ITN, but only rarely does he discriminate publicly between 'good' and 'bad' journalism. In most of his speeches there is an attack at some point on the 'media' – often his remarks seem to act as 'warm-up' material to get the crowd going, and also, if television cameras are present, to give it something on which to vent its anger. Scargill has admitted that to some extent his criticism is deliberately designed to keep journalists 'on their toes' and to make them constantly question what they are doing. In this, his criticisms have had some effect:

journalists have begun to think more carefully about how they present industrial matters. At the same time it may have contributed to the hostility, sometimes leading to physical attacks, that journalists, and particularly television crews, have suffered on miners' picket lines.

Like many people of high dynamism, determination and competence, Scargill can find it difficult to play second fiddle. 'It is difficult to see him being Vice-President of anything,' says one man who worked with him in the Yorkshire Left. Perhaps the best example of this is in the TUC, which Scargill has never been keen on. In 1983 he even gave up his place on the TUC General Council. With the reorganization of the General Council the number of NUM places dropped from two to one, and the TUC rejected a Scargill plan to restore to the NUM its second place. So he left the Council, and allowed McGahey to remain, arguing that he had always believed in 'collective leadership'.

But Scargill has never got on well with the TUC. He was annoyed with the 'Buggin's turn' principle which kept him off the important sub-committees, and during three years on the General Council he had a poor attendance record. At one point, in 1982, Scargill began seriously questioning the usefulness of the TUC and even discussed the idea of forming an alternative, left-wing, breakaway TUC.[10] In 1984 it was several months before Scargill formally approached the TUC for help in the miners' dispute, and yet at Saltley, his greatest hour, he admitted that victory could not have been achieved without the help of other unions. In 1984 Scargill distrusted the TUC after what he saw as its 'sell-out' over the NGA and GCHQ disputes, and he didn't want them to force a compromise settlement on the miners. It was only after long persuasion by close colleagues that Scargill agreed to approach the TUC General Council just before the 1984 Brighton Congress, and agree on a statement to Congress.

Earlier, in 1983, Scargill successfully proposed that the NUM disaffiliate from the Miners' International Federation (MIF), which comprises only Western mining unions, in order that he could help set up a mining federation involving mining unions from both East and West. The decision was particularly annoying to his former political ally from Yorkshire Peter Tait, who had left the NUM Executive and the Communist Party to become the Miners' International Federation General Secretary. Tait says he only knew about the NUM's move when he read about it in the *Financial Times*. As a result of the British disaffiliation the MIF has become severely weakened. Its headquarters is being moved to Brussels and Tait has decided to give up his job. Tait argues on the basis of what happened in both the TUC and the MIF that if Scargill 'hasn't built the organization he's not prepared to play in it – be it the TUC or the Miners' International Federation'.[11]

It is a frequent criticism of Scargill that, unlike other trade union leaders, he is not a 'negotiator', but Scargill himself would probably take it as a compliment. Other union leaders, such as David Basnett, Ron Todd, Moss Evans and Terry Duffy, made the way to the leadership of their unions by being highly successful 'negotiators'. But Scargill's road to the top was more of a political route: he succeeded by making himself known and popular, by getting his policies across, and through good organization. None of Scargill's positions in the NUM has involved much negotiating work. Branch delegate is a political representative role – any negotiations are usually left to the branch secretary. The job of Compensation Agent does require negotiating skills but is much more a matter of presenting legal claims and arguing legal points rather than striking bargains. Even as Yorkshire President Scargill would not have done much negotiation. In a large area such as Yorkshire, most disputes are negotiated by the four area agents.

A leading member of the NUM Executive argues that Scargill negotiates as if he was going along a railway track: 'when he hits the buffers he jumps off the rails, and is totally lost, whereas Gormley would switch from track to track, and take on new issues. At the end of the day he would squeeze something out of them. Whereas all Scargill gets is a series of "Noes". I've been involved in negotiations with Scargill where I knew that I on my own could have got something out of the Board, but because of the way he approached them we got nowhere, and they could hardly then concede points to me when they had already turned down the President.'

A senior Coal Board negotiator agrees with that assessment: 'He's like Perry Mason. He carries out his brief to the letter, but when he gets beyond that, he's lost.'

Another NCB man who knew Scargill in Yorkshire argues: 'If you say "I'm going to have what I want", like he does, that's not negotiating. He's not even a good strategist.'

But Scargill would argue that for other union leaders, and for former leaders of the NUM, the term 'negotiation' has so often meant 'compromise' or 'sell-out'. He feels that too often in the past miners' leaders have been too willing to compromise and negotiate things away unnecessarily, rather than stand firm. On the day he announced his election campaign, in May 1981, he made his position quite clear: 'If the price of winning the presidency is to compromise my views or compromise my principles then you can keep the job.'[12]

In many ways Arthur Scargill is as much a politician as he is a trade union leader, and, indeed, it has been suggested that he might one day enter politics. Scargill claims that he has been offered four Parliamentary seats in his time. Nobody has it in his or her power to 'offer' anybody a Labour seat, but there is little doubt that Scargill could easily have become a Labour candidate if he had wanted. Scargill turned the 'offers' down, arguing that he had more power as a union leader than he would have as an MP. 'I can pick up the phone here and get things done. An MP can't do that, can he.'[13]

He is a brilliant political operator, able to react quickly to events and to survive in the political jungle. Colleagues from the Yorkshire Left recall his statistical expertise and how he could calculate the way the votes from each NUM branch would divide. When it came to elections, some recall, Scargill would prepare meticulously, leaving nothing to chance.

Scargill prefers to pursue his political aims through the trade union movement. It is impossible, however, to attach any political label to him – Stalinist, Leninist, Trotskyist, New Left Socialist. At one stage Scargill was quite happy to call himself a Marxist, but now he rarely describes himself as such. This may be for pragmatic reasons rather than because of any change in his attitudes. Certainly his more recent statements are entirely compatible with a Marxist view of the world: 'Free enterprise based upon exploitation produces waste and decay and cannot hope to survive. There is no moral or political justification for its continuation and there are very powerful arguments for it to be overthrown before its own inevitable collapse.'[14]

Unlike many socialists, the remarkable thing about Scargill is the consistency of his views over the years. Speeches made twenty years ago could easily have been delivered today. His views seem to have been largely moulded during his time in the Young Communist League.

Perhaps the best description of him is simply that he is a Scargillite. Unlike most politicians Scargill rarely quotes somebody else on a subject to support his views. He prefers to decide on his policies for himself, without using the texts of other socialist thinkers. His views roughly correspond to those of the 'Bennite' far-Left. He would agree with them on many issues – the need for more nationalization, import controls, restoring spending cuts, getting rid of nuclear weapons, cuts in arms spending, withdrawal from the EEC, opposition to incomes policy, Labour Party democracy, among other issues. But there are other important matters on which he is out of tune with most of the Labour far-Left.

For instance, Scargill seems to have little time for some aspects of modern feminism. He defended the right of Maurice Jones to publish pin-ups of scantily clad women in the *Yorkshire Miner*, and he feels it is not unnatural that his wife should do most of the domestic work at home, like cooking and ironing: 'I couldn't imagine being with anyone who was too busy to do those things. That sort of career woman wouldn't last with me.'[15] On the other hand, during the 1984 strike Scargill encouraged miners' wives to see the dispute as their fight as much as their husbands', and his wife, Anne, played a leading role in the miners' support groups.

Scargill has been a firm advocate of proportional representation (PR) all his life. PR is still unfashionable on the Left, especially in the Labour Party (although it is an issue which unites the SDP/Liberal Alliance and the Communist Party). At times Scargill seems to go out of his way to stress his belief in it: '[I] fail to understand how any person who claims to be a democrat can oppose it ... You cannot have an argument in favour of democracy without having an argument in favour of proportional representation which secures a government elected by a majority of people.'[16]

Eastern Europe is another issue on which Scargill would fall out with many on the Left, although here his attitudes do seem to be neither consistently pro-Soviet nor anti-Soviet.

After visits to Eastern Europe he has been very dismissive of the way of life in those countries – 'If this is Communism, they can keep it,' he is reported to have said after a holiday in Bulgaria (albeit by the *Sun*): 'If this is an advertisement for international socialism, they will create more capitalists than I've ever seen.'[17]

He has been highly critical of Solidarity in Poland, describing it in September 1983 as 'an anti-socialist organization' (Solidarity nevertheless gave its support to the 1984 strike). At other times, however, Scargill has been strongly critical of the Soviet attitude towards trade unions.

He says he supported the Soviet invasion of Hungary in 1956, but not that of Czechoslovakia in 1968. He feels the Hungarian uprising was organized by the CIA, whereas the 'Prague spring' was, he believes, a 'popular uprising' channelled towards a 'rethink of socialism'.[18]

In interviews Scargill has also criticized the Soviet treatment of dissidents who he believes should be allowed to leave their country if they wish. Yet, when he is asked by pressure groups to support protests about particular Soviet dissidents, he seems to take little interest. A Yorkshire miner who wrote to Scargill about two Russian miners who had been arrested for campaigning for independent trade unions was told: 'The people who constantly inundate this office with letters about the above two people do not appear to show any concern, or very little concern about the tragedy of El Salvador and Nicaragua where more people are dying in a day than have ever been killed in the Soviet Union in the past ten years.'[19]

Cuba seems to come nearest to Scargill's idea of a model socialist state. He has visited it several times and has twice met Fidel Castro. He regards Cuba as 'a 100 per cent improvement on what you have in the Soviet Union'.[20]

Another issue where Scargill disagrees with many on the Left is the question of 'workers' control', and giving employees a say in the running of their companies. He vehemently opposes it:

It is the apologists' alternative to socialism ... I firmly believe that the struggle in our society today can only be advanced by putting into operation the principle and the concept of free collective bargaining ... There has to be a recognition that the trade union movement, through its normal processes of free collective bargaining, can bring about the changes that we want to see, even under the present system. The only time we can really have workers' control is under a socialist system of society. I reject the argument that you can have some kind of workers' control within capitalism. What you *can* have is class collaboration within capitalism ... Once we've put workers on the boards they become bureaucrats ... those who actually sit on the boards of directors ... begin to think with a completely different outlook from when they were workers' representatives.[21]

For Scargill, workers' control is a palliative which distracts from the 'mass struggle' which he believes necessary to bring about a socialist society. It blurs the distinction between those who rule and those who are ruled those who own and those who are owned.

Scargill's political philosophy is all about giving leadership. He sees it as his duty to increase the political awareness of his members, to 'politicize' them, by communicating with them in a way that they will understand and respond to, and on issues they are concerned about: 'We have to begin a programme of re-education, and I don't say that in an academic or abstract sense. The fundamental weakness of our movement is that we don't have a politicisation of working-class people ... When we can persuade the mass of working people to accept an alternative radical programme, only then will we be able to move toward a Socialist system of society.'[22]

His belief in proportional representation can be understood in that light. Scargill believes that with PR the Left would be forced to go out and sell itself to the electorate, and he is confident that it could achieve a majority vote. His own personal election campaigns have proved to him the success of intense campaigning on socialist issues, and each time he achieved landslide victories.

In Yorkshire that leadership and politicization campaign involved two notable elements – setting up the *Yorkshire Miner*, and creating many more places on university day release courses.

But Scargill believes leadership involves communicating with people on issues where they will respond, as he explained to *New Left Review* in 1975: 'There have been tremendous strides forward in Yorkshire in the miners' union. It's been done because we have a left-progressive leadership that has been willing to stand up and say "no" to the Coal Board ... It's precisely because that sort of leadership has been given on the question of wages and conditions that we have won support ... It is precisely because of our experience that we have the miners involved in protest marches [and] demonstrations ... You would never have got this six years ago. For it's the influence of militant leadership, a result of positive leadership, given in a situation where the miners can see, day by day, where we are and what we are doing. They don't want to see anybody going onto a platform and yelling: "I am a Marxist and I want to see dialectical materialism being brought in as the order of the day." They couldn't care bloody less but ... they could care what's in their wage packet on a Friday, they could care about what their conditions are like. The very fact of being able to achieve all that we have won with Marxist, progressive, left-wing leadership strengthens our movement.'[23]

Scargill rejects the 'purity' of much of the ultra-Left. For him it is more important to win people over to socialism than to win obscure and ideological points of principle. He sees no reason, for example, why 'socialist newspapers have got to be drab and dreary'. Hence the attractive style of Yorkshire Miner and The Miner: 'There is no reason why we can't write our stories in a popular fresh way that will appeal, particularly to young people who don't normally read about politics.'[24]

For Scargill, as for many on the Left, there is no distinction between political and industrial struggles. They are all part of the same battles: 'Trade unions are political; their role is to bring about political change as much as industrial change.'[25]

Scargill believes that a dispute like the 1984 miners' strike cannot be treated in isolation from wider political issues: 'We want to save our jobs. But more – we want to prepare the way for a transformation, rolling back the years of Thatcherism. We want to pave the way for an economic recovery, a general election and the return of a Labour government.'[26]

How great is Scargill's commitment to a change of government by democratic means? Scargill insists that he does believe in the Parliamentary process, but that Parliament alone cannot be relied upon to bring about change: 'Anybody who believes that we shall achieve socialism simply by electing a number of MPs is deluding themselves ... Parliaments do not necessarily reflect the views of ordinary people, and if you have a Parliament that is not being pushed by a working-class movement demanding, expecting and requiring change, then you will not get that change ... I believe that we can bring about a political change through Parliament, but only if it's backed by mass mobilisation of ordinary working people desirous of change. If we do that we've got the basis for a real revolutionary change in British politics that I want to see ...'[27]

Scargill's former friend, turned critic, Jimmy Reid, said that having known Scargill for twenty-five years he is convinced Scargill considers himself to be 'Britain's Lenin': 'Scargillism ... is based on seizing power, not winning it through the democratic process. Arthur's contempt for democracy is manifest.'[28]

Many people suggested that his refusal to hold a national ballot in 1984 was clearly a sign of contempt for democracy. And yet it is difficult to say Scargill is totally contemptuous of democracy, as Reid does, when he believes so fervently in proportional representation, and when he believes so fervently in the need to campaign to change people's attitudes. Scargill's rise within the NUM has largely been the result of campaigns and politicization, not of conspiracies and backroom wheeling and dealing. The men who met in the Albert Club decided to go out and win support among the Yorkshire members.

But Scargill's view of political change is at least ambiguous. After the Saltley picket in 1972 he said that if another situation like Saltley occurred in future 'then the whole picture can change from one where you have a peaceful road to one where you do not have such a peaceful road'.[29]

Some would argue that comments like that, together with his talk of overthrowing governments and his refusal to condemn picket-line violence, are signs that Scargill would not object to violence as a means of bringing about the revolutionary change he wants – provided he thought it would be successful. According to this argument, Scargill sees Parliamentary democracy as just one of a number of possible roads to socialism.

Privately, Scargill probably dislikes much of the indiscriminate violence which occurred in 1984 the stone-throwing and vandalism carried out by some pickets. He sees such acts as unnecessary and undisciplined. For Scargill the General, a disciplined, sober 'army' is vital. Indiscipline in the ranks makes him very angry. On the other hand, he understands why such actions come about, and he could never condemn such actions in public because that would be betraying the men on the picket lines. Although in late November Scargill did condemn attacks on working miners' homes.

What kind of socialist society would Scargill want to bring about? It would be one where all the means of production would be brought into public state ownership: 'In the initial stages there may be one or two small private firms, but towards the end of a developing period, when we've got socialism, I would have thought there's no need for people to own and control industries ... though there would of course be the right of every individual to own their own home and own their own garden ...'[30]

The economy of Scargill's socialist Britain would be totally planned, and would include an incomes policy: 'the wages of workers – mineworkers or any other section of the working class – would be determined on the basis of discussion within the central system.'[31]

Unions, though, would retain the right to strike: 'I think that any system that is established that removes the worker's right to withdraw his or her labour is anti-democratic and should not be tolerated and that's why I condemn many of the East European states.'[32]

But Scargill also believes that in a system without class conflict the role of the unions would be different. Similarly, Parliament would continue to exist, along with opposition parties. Their role, though, would be much reduced: 'I would hope that the sort of system that operated ... would eventually reach the stage where the opposition party would play a very little part ... my philosophy suggests to me that a political party represents a class of people ... if you establish a system where there is only one owning and controlling class, then the need for the sort of opposition that we are talking about now ... would no longer exist.'[33]

Scargill says he is a Christian, and as such has a 'tremendous belief' in human beings: 'I know that we can produce a society where man will cease to simply go to work and have a little leisure, but will release his latent talent and ability and begin to produce in the cultural sense all the things that I know he's capable of: music, poetry, writing, sculpture, whole works of art that, at the moment, are literally lying dormant simply because we, as a society, are not able to tap it.'[34]

Conclusion

A lot of people have already said that in some ways I remind them of A. J. Cook. I think that Cook was probably the greatest leader the miners ever produced. To be talked about in the same breath is a tribute. I would like to think that I could in some way measure up in part to the kind of leader that Cook was in the Miners' Federation of Great Britain. If in part I can do that I shall think that I've done my job very well indeed.

– Arthur Scargill, 1979[1]

On 28 September the 1984 strike reached its two-hundredth day – the longest national strike in the history of the British trade union movement. After nearly a hundred hours of negotiations a settlement between the two sides looked no nearer. The 'drift back to work', upon which the Coal Board had pinned its hopes during the summer, was still going slowly. On the other hand, in spite of promises made at the TUC Congress at Brighton, there was little sign of other unions taking the kind of industrial action they had in 1972 and 1974, and which they had so readily promised in 1981. More working days had been lost than in any British industrial dispute for almost sixty years. By the middle of October the 1984 strike had gone on longer than the lock-out of 1926.

There are similarities between 1926 and 1984. Both disputes started in the spring – the worst time of year for a strike from the miners' point of view. In both cases a determined Conservative government claimed to be standing aside, but gave its full support to the employers. In both 1926 and 1984 the miners received only limited support from the rest of the labour movement: in 1926 the General Strike lasted only nine days; in 1984 the TUC unions gave little help to the NUM in terms of industrial action. On both occasions the miners of Nottinghamshire wrecked the miners' solidarity. And in both cases the miners were led by young, dynamic, incorruptible left-wing leaders who were personally identified with the dispute: in 1926 it was A. J. Cook, in 1984 Arthur Scargill.

Cook and Scargill have a lot in common. Cook was only forty-two in 1926, four years younger than Scargill in 1984, and had become leader of the Miners' Federation only two years earlier. Cook was a revolutionary socialist who believed that society could be changed by industrial unionism, rather than through Parliament, and that unions could abolish the capitalist system. At one time he had been a member of the Communist Party, but he largely remained independent from party politics.

By all accounts Cook was an even better speaker than Scargill: he too needed no notes, and his great oratory roused many audiences. During 1926 he worked himself to exhaustion, travelling the coalfields on speaking tours, keeping up the spirits of his members. When there were signs of a drift back to work anywhere, a speech from Cook would often keep many men out. But in 1926 Cook soon believed the miners had to compromise and entered into secret negotiations.

After the failure of 1926 Cook was a tragic, broken man, who felt personal responsibility for the miners' humiliation. In time he became a more moderate leader, and was accused of selling out. His health had long been in decline, and in November 1931 he died, at the age of forty-seven.

Scargill looks upon A. J. Cook as one of his heroes, but it is unlikely that he will suffer the same fate. During 1984 Scargill showed no signs of flagging, and no signs of compromise.

When the inquests into the 1984 dispute are held by the NUM, Scargill may not come out well. On several issues in 1984 his judgement seems to have been seriously lacking, and even his strongest supporters admit he made mistakes. It was wrong to allow pickets into areas before they had held a ballot. Whatever the rights and wrongs of starting the strike under the area-by-area rule, Rule 41, it was tactically foolish not to hold a national ballot during the early weeks of the dispute. Other actions which may be held against him are his decision not to approach the TUC until August and the failure to reach a settlement in negotiations.

It could be argued that Scargill's professionalism on television had suffered from his appearing too frequently and from his being too aggressive. Scargill's determination to keep repeating simple points got to the stage where his audience became bored – at hearing for instance that 'Britain produces the deepest cheap-mined coal in the world'. His refusal to condemn violence on the picket lines contrasted strongly with some left-wing NUM branch officials who were prepared to condemn such violence, but who also argued that it was the result of miners' frustration and that much of the violence had been carried out by outside agitators. Their case was much more convincing than Scargill's, which usually refused to acknowledge even that any violence by miners had taken place. And his personalized attacks on Ian MacGregor did little to help the NUM cause (but then nor did MacGregor's personal attacks on Scargill help the NCB).

The contacts with Libya, revealed by the *Sunday Times* in October, were heavily criticized by colleagues, even on the Left (among them Jack Taylor), not only because they considered the decision to approach Libya itself to be wrong, but because Scargill told so few people about it. The episode illustrated Scargill's highly personalized leadership. Although throughout he had the support of the NUM Executive and Conference for the principle of the strike, by running it in such an autocratic manner, he was bound to be heavily associated with the outcome. As the return to work reached significant numbers in November, and Christmas approaching, that outcome looked increasingly like defeat for the NUM.

Scargill can be President of the NUM until he is sixty-five in the year 2003. In future, NUM officials have to stand for election every five years, but the rules were changed after Scargill's election in 1981. Scargill strongly supported the change and said he would not object to standing for re-election every five years. It will be interesting therefore to see if he offers himself for re-election in 1986. If he chooses not to, constitutionally he could be removed by the NUM Conference, but, with its present composition, such a decision is unlikely.

It is more likely that other left-wing members of the NUM Executive will try to keep a firmer grip on Scargill in future. In particular, Peter Heathfield may choose to assert himself more. Constitutionally the NUM Secretary is equal in status to the President, and before Joe Gormley the post was traditionally more important.

Whatever the outcome of 1984, further confrontations between the miners and the Government look inevitable. If 1984 is seen to be a victory for the NUM, it will give the union a new confidence, and will be seen to justify militant action and a refusal to compromise. And there are other battles to be fought – on pay, shorter working hours, holidays and earlier retirement. Victory would give Arthur Scargill himself hero-status within the labour movement, making him a focus for opposition to the more right-wing leadership of the TUC and the Labour Party.

The strike has also shown miners that they can survive without pay, or much income from state benefits, for much longer than almost any of them would have predicted beforehand. The miners' support groups enabled the miners to survive without money and boosted community morale. And after a while many miners said they didn't want to go back to work, quite apart from the reasons for the strike.

If 1984 is seen as a defeat, pits will be closed on the grounds that they are uneconomic, and probably on a far larger scale than originally intended. Scargill will want that defeat avenged, but it may be many years before his membership is prepared to back him.

But, whatever the outcome, after so long on strike the miners will be in no mood for further industrial action for a long time to come. It will take years for miners to repay the debts they have accumulated in 1984. Some miners were still paying the debts they had accumulated at the Co-op during the 1926 dispute long after the Second World War.

The NUM will be a more polarized and divided union once the strike is over. The areas in which miners mainly carried on working in 1984 are likely to elect more right-wing representatives in future. Several leading area officials are due to retire over the next few years. The wholesale clear-out of left-wing branch officials in Nottinghamshire in 1984 may be repeated in areas such as Staffordshire, South Derbyshire, the Midlands and Lancashire. It could lead to more right-wing members of the Executive. In the Nottingham area, for instance, Ray Chadburn and Henry Richardson, who both supported the strike, may be replaced as Executive members by two full-time officials who supported the working miners, Roy Lynk and David Prendergast. Even in Yorkshire, leading left-wingers fear a right-wing backlash in the next branch elections, which were postponed from June 1984.

The machinery which the Right and the anti-Scargill movement could use, now exists – because of the dispute. The working miners' associations are now organized, though it is difficult to see them ever becoming a majority. The National Working Miners' Committee says it will continue to exist after the strike, and will back 'sensible' candidates in future elections. It may act in a similar way as the Left's own unofficial organizations worked so successfully in the late 1960s and the 1970s. But the working miners will find it difficult to succeed simply on a negative, anti-Scargill platform: they will need to offer positive alternatives.

The recent trend has been for the NUM Executive to move to the Left. Most of the new recruits to the Executive have been noticeably more left wing than the men they replaced. The imminent closure of Haig Colliery in Cumberland will kill off that area altogether. Furthermore, the Left have been trying for some time to reduce the over-representation of the NUM's smaller sections on the Executive. These areas are predominantly right wing, and the possibility of amalgamating some of these sections is under review. Arthur Scargill has long argued for voting strengths on the

Executive to reflect membership. Such moves would undoubtedly favour the Left, but it will be difficult for the leadership to get the necessary two-thirds majority at NUM Conference to make the changes.

But the consequences of the union's divisions in 1984 could be even more serious. Already there are pressures for some areas to leave the NUM – for instance, in Trevor Bell's Colliery Officials and Staffs Area. Use of the NUM's new disciplinary procedures – the so-called 'Star Chambers' – after the strike would certainly precipitate more legal cases, and could even provoke a major split within the union. If the NUM expelled Chris Butcher ('Silver Birch') from the union, for instance, he might be supported by thousands of other miners. That could lead to the start of a breakaway miners' union: again the working miners' committees and their funds could provide the basis for such a union, although the committees themselves vehemently deny that they wish to leave the NUM. It should not be forgotten, however, that George Spencer only formed his union in 1926 after he had been expelled from the Miners' Federation conference.

Even if the NUM does survive intact, which is still the more likely outcome, the bitterness between those men who went on strike in 1984 and those who worked will last for generations.

In 1956 the members of the miners' Union Jack Memorial Club in Goldthorpe, South Yorkshire, were asked to vote on whether they would readmit to membership miners who had returned to work early in 1926. They had been blacked by the club ever since. Thirty years later, long after many of the 1926 strikers were dead, the Goldthorpe miners voted by ninety votes to thirty-six not to readmit the 1926 'scabs'.

Miners have long memories.

Appendix

Extracts from the N U M Rule-Book
Rules 41 and 43

As at 1 March 1984

STRIKES AND LOCK-OUTS

41. – In the event of a dispute arising in any Area or applying to the workers in any Branch likely or possible to lead to a stoppage of work or any other industrial action short of a strike the questions involved must be immediately reported by the appropriate official of the Area in question to the National Executive Committee which shall deal with the matter forthwith, and in no case shall a cessation of work or other form of industrial action short of a strike take place by the workers without the previous sanction of the National Executive Committee, or of a Committee (whether consisting of members of the National Executive Committee or of other persons) to whom the National Executive Committee may have delegated the power of giving such sanction, either generally or in a particular case and no funds of the Union shall be applied in strike pay or other trades dispute benefit for the benefit of workers who shall have ceased work without the previous sanction of the National Executive Committee.

NATIONAL ACTION

43. – In the event of national action being proposed by the Union in pursuance of any of the objects of the Union, the following provision shall apply:

That a national strike shall only be entered upon as the result of a ballot vote of the members taken in pursuance of a resolution of Conference, and a strike shall not be declared unless 55 per cent* of those voting in the ballot vote in favour of such a strike. If a ballot vote be taken during the time a strike is in progress, a vote of 55 per cent* of those taking part in the ballot shall be necessary to continue the strike.

If a ballot vote be taken during the time a stoppage is in progress, such stoppage may not be continued unless 55 per cent* of those voting in the ballot vote in favour of continuance.

* The words '55 per cent' were replaced by the words 'a simple majority' at the Special Conference on 19 April 1984.

Notes

INTRODUCTION

1. J. Wake, interview with D. Akerman.
2. The term 'The Enemy Within' had in fact been used by the *Daily Express* in its front-page headline almost a year earlier, on 29 August 1983, in reference to both Arthur Scargill and Ken Livingstone. Scargill had just said in Moscow that Britain and America were the biggest threat to world peace.
3. Figures quoted from the Department of Employment New Earnings Survey and quoted in J. Hughes and R. Moore (eds.), *A Special Case?*, p. 25, Penguin, Harmondsworth, 1972. This book publishes the NUM evidence to the Wilberforce Court of Inquiry, which broadly accepted the NUM's figures. Wilberforce acknowledged that miners had fallen from the top rank of the pay league down to the middle.

CHAPTER I: The Scot Who Went to Barnsley

1. Lord Robens, *Ten Year Stint*, p. 12, Cassell, London, 1972.
2. F. Watters, interview with the author.
3. A. Taylor, *The Politics of the Yorkshire Miners*, p. 32, Croom Helm, London, 1984. I am greatly indebted to Taylor's work, and to his advice and cooperation, for much of this chapter.
4. See B. J. McCormick, 'Strikes in the Yorkshire Coalfield, 1947–1963', in D. Forsyth and D. Kelly (eds.), *Studies in the British Coal Industry*, Pergamon, Oxford, 1969.
5. Ministry of Labour, *Written Evidence to the Royal Commission on Trade Unions and Employers' Associations*, p. 39, HMSO, London, 1965, quoted in B. J. McCormick, op. cit.
6. B. J. McCormick, op. cit.
7. Quoted in P. Kahn, 'An Interview with Frank Watters', *Society for the Study of Labour History Bulletin*, 43, Autumn 1981.
8. D. Baines, interview with the author.

9. G. Wilkinson, interview with D. Akerman.

10. Vic Allen, in his *The Militancy of British Miners*, Moor Press, Shipley, 1981, deals with some of the work of the Yorkshire Left. See also the interview with Tommy Mullany by P. Kahn, *Society for the Study of Labour History Bulletin*, 45, Autumn 1982.

11. J. Oldham, interview with D. Akerman.

12. F. Watters, interview with the author.

CHAPTER 2: The Boy Who Would Be King

1. A. Scargill, 'The New Unionism' (interview), *New Left Review*, 92, July/August 1975, p. 3.

2. Ibid., pp. 4–5.

3. Quoted in J. Mortimer, *In Character*, pp. 63–4, Penguin, Harmondsworth, 1984.

4. Quoted in the *Illustrated London News*, July 1978.

5. Quoted in the *Observer*, 3 February 1974.

6. A. Scargill, interview for TV-am, 14 December 1983.

7. Dorothy Bamford, quoted in the *Observer Magazine*, 17 June 1979.

8. *Illustrated London News* (see note 4).

9. J. Mortimer, op. cit., p. 63.

10. Ibid.

11. *New Left Review* (see note 1), p. 3.

12. *New Left Review* (see note 1) p. 4.

13. J. Mortimer, op. cit., p. 65.

14. *New Left Review* (see note 1), p. 4.

15. Quoted in the *Daily Mirror*, 25 November 1980.

16. J. Mortimer, op. cit., p. 65.

17. Quoted in the *Observer Magazine*, 17 June 1979.

18. Quoted in the *Daily Mail*, 10 December 1974.

19. Quoted in the *Observer*, 3 February 1974.

20. Quoted in the *Daily Mail*, 10 December 1974.

21. Account of BBC 1 *Person to Person* interview, the *Listener*, 9 August 1979.

22. J. Mortimer, op. cit., p. 63.

23. *Challenge*, 23 April 1955.

24. Jean Miller, quoted in the *Daily Mail*, 9 December 1977.

25. *Person to Person* (see note 21).

26. Account of BBC 2 *Newsday* interview, the *Listener*, 23 October 1975.

27. J. Mortimer, op. cit., p. 65.

28. *New Left Review* (see note 1), p. 5.

29. *Challenge*, June 1957.

30. Quoted in the *Daily Mail*, 9 December 1977.
31. A. Scargill, election manifesto, Worsbrough Urban District Council elections, 14 May 1960 (see the *Observer Magazine*, 17 June 1979).
32. *Newsday* (see note 27).
33. Quoted in the *Daily Mirror*, 25 November 1980.
34. Quoted in *The Times*, 28 November 1977.
35. Quoted in the *Daily Express*, 17 October 1977.
36. J. Mortimer, op. cit., p. 66.
37. *Newsday* (see note 27).
38. Quoted in the *Observer Magazine*, 17 June 1979.
39. Including in a conversation with the author, in August 1984, when Scargill said one could not be a member of both the YCL and the Party.
40. F. Watters, interview with the author.
41. Quoted in the *Sunday Times*, 17 November 1974.
42. *New Left Review* (see note 1), p. 6.

CHAPTER 3: Adventurers and Splinter Groups

1. Lord Robens, *Ten Year Stint*, p. 24, Cassell, London, 1972.
2. P. Tait, interview with the author.
3. V. L. Allen, *The Militancy of British Miners*, Moor Press, Shipley, 1981.
4. A. Taylor, *The Politics of the Yorkshire Miners*, p. 6, Croom Helm, London, 1984.
5. Quoted in V. L. Allen, op. cit., p. 156.
6. A. Scargill, 'The New Unionism' (interview), *New Left Review*, 92, July/August 1975, pp. 9–10.
7. Ibid., p. 11.
8. J. Miller, interview with the author.
9. R. Rigby, interview with the author.
10. NUM Annual Conference Report, 1970, pp. 137–9.
11. Ibid., pp. 87–8.
12. J. Gormley, *Battered Cherub*, p. 76, Hamish Hamilton, London, 1982.
13. *New Left Review* (see note 6), p. 11.
14. Ibid.
15. Ibid.
16. V. L. Allen, op. cit., p. 140.
17. A. Mitchell, interview with the author.

CHAPTER 4: The Battle of Saltley Gate

1. A. Scargill, 'The New Unionism' (interview), *New Left Review*, 92, July/August 1975, p. 13.

2. A. Scargill, interview, for TV-am, 14 December 1983.
3. Quoted in R. Taylor, *The Fifth Estate*, p. 362, Pan, London, 1980.
4. *New Left Review* (see note 1), p. 13.
5. D. Baines, interview with the author.
6. *New Left Review* (see note 1), p. 12.
7. Ibid.
8. R. Rigby, interview with the author.
9. Ibid.
10. *Birmingham Evening Mail*, 3 February 1972.
11. *Birmingham Evening Mail*, 4 February 1972.
12. F. Watters, Granada TV, *World in Action*, 15 October 1984.
13. *New Left Review* (see note 1), p. 15.
14. *Birmingham Evening Mail*, 7 February 1972.
15. Account of Scargill's speech given by F. Watters in an interview with the author.
16. *New Left Review* (see note 1), p. 18.
17. Ex-Chief-Supt. A. Brannigan, interview with the author.
18. *Birmingham Evening Mail*, 10 February 1972.
19. Quoted on ATV news, 10 February 1972.
20. *New Left Review* (see note 1), p. 17.
21. It was also in the 1972 coal dispute that David Owen, then a Labour MP, put pickets up at his home in Limehouse.
22. F. Watters, *World in Action* (see note 12).
23. Ex-Chief-Supt. A. Brannigan, interview with the author.
24. D. Beavis, interview with the author.
25. D. Hurd, *An End to Promises*, p. 103, Collins, London, 1979.
26. T. Bell, interview with the author.
27. G. Wilkinson, interview with D. Akerman.
28. F. Watters, *World in Action* (see note 12).
29. *The Times*, 25 September 1972.
30. Quoted in *The Times*, 3 January 1974.
31. *New Left Review* (see note 1), p. 21.

CHAPTER 5: Camelot

1. Quoted in the *Sunday Times*, 17 November 1974.
2. B. Hines, *The Price of Coal*, Hutchinson, London, 1979.
3. Report of the Compensation Agent for 1976, Yorkshire Area NUM, 1976.
4. I. Ross, interview with the author.
5. H. Wilson, *Final Term: The Labour Government 1974–1976*, p. 116, Weidenfeld and Nicolson, London, 1979.

6. Quoted in the *Sunday Times*, 17 November 1974.
7. V. L. Allen, *The Militancy of British Miners*, p. 290, Moor Press, Shipley, 1981.
8. *Morning Star*, 26 September 1974.
9. *The Miner*, December 1974.
10. Quoted in the *Financial Times*, 17 April 1984.
11. Quoted in *The Times*, 23 June 1977.
12. Quoted in J. Dromey and G. Taylor, *Grunwick: The Workers' Story* p. 141, Lawrence and Wishart, London, 1978.
13. Ibid., p. 123.
14. Quoted in the *Daily Telegraph*, 18 July 1977.
15. NUM Annual Conference Report, 1978.
16. P. Tait, interview with the author.
17. Much of this section is based in the work of Andrew Taylor. See his: (i) *The Politics of the Yorkshire Miners*, Croom Helm, London, 1984; (ii) 'The Modern Boroughmongers? The Yorkshire Area (NUM) and Grassroots Politics', *Political Studies*, 33, 1984; (iii) Paper of similar title, presented to the Annual Conference of the Political Studies Association, Canterbury, 1982; (iv) 'Yorkshire miners gun for Mason', *New Statesman*, 30 November 1979 (with J. MacFarlane).

CHAPTER 6: The Road to Cortonwood

1. Quoted in the *Daily Telegraph*, 13 February 1981.
2. Yorkshire Area NUM ballot paper, 29–30 January 1981.
3. J. Taylor, interview with D. Akerman.
4. *Daily Telegraph*, 16 February 1981.
5. *Daily Telegraph*, 17 February 1981.
6. D. Howell, interview with ITN Channel 4 News, recorded 14 November 1984.
7. *Marxism Today*, April 1981.
8. J. Gormley, *Battered Cherub*, p. 207, Hamish Hamilton, London, 1982.
9. Ibid.
10. *Guardian*, 1 December 1981.
11. Quoted in *The Times*, 9 December 1981.
12. *Daily Express*, 13 January 1982.
13. Quoted in *The Times*, 19 January 1982.
14. *Daily Express*, 9 December 1981.
15. Quoted in the *Daily Telegraph*, 25 June 1982.
16. Quoted in *The Times*, 6 July 1982.
17. Quoted in the *Sunday Times*, 31 October 1982.
18. Quoted in *The Times*, 1 March 1983.
19. Quoted in *The Times*, 2 March 1983.

20. *The Miner*, special edition, March 1983.
21. NUM Annual Conference Report, July 1983.
22. Ibid.
23. Ibid.
24. A MORI poll for the *Sunday Times* taken on 13 January showed that 35 per cent thought the ban should be called off, while 61 per cent said it shouldn't.
25. J. Taylor, interview with D. Akerman.
26. G. Hayes, interview with D. Akerman.
27. J. Wake, interview with D. Akerman.

CHAPTER 7: Pickets and Ballots

1. Quoted in *The Times*, 7 March 1984.
2. Minutes of the Yorkshire Area NUM Executive, 7 March 1984.
3. Quoted in *The Times*, 7 March 1984.
4. MORI poll for LWT *Weekend World*, taken 9 March 1984 among 969 miners at sixty-two pits.
5. Letter from P. Heathfield to T. Bell, 21 March 1984.
6. Letter from P. Heathfield to J. Jones, 26 March 1984.
7. Quoted in *The Times*, 28 March 1984.
8. NUM Special Conference Report, 19 April 1984.
9. Apart from the 9 March LWT poll (see note 4), these were as follows: (i) NOP poll, 30 March, showed 51 per cent to 34 per cent, with 15 per cent others; (ii) ORC-Harris poll for LWT *Weekend World*, taken 12–14 April, showed 55 per cent for a strike, 33 per cent against; (iii) ORC-Harris poll for ITN, taken 21–2 May, showed 65 per cent to 28 per cent; (iv) ORC-Harris poll for ITN Channel 4 News, taken 7–8 July, showed 61 per cent to 29 per cent.
10. See *The Economist*, 27 May 1978.

CHAPTER 8: Land of the Silver Birch

1. A. Fearn, interview with the author.
2. *Daily Express*, 9 August 1984.
3. A. Fearn, interview with the author.
4. Ibid.
5. William Carter, quoted in A. Griffin, *The Miners of Nottinghamshire: 1914–1944*, p. 176, Allen and Unwin, London, 1962.
6. Minutes of the Rufford branch of the NMIU.
7. G. Jelley, interview with the author for ITN Channel 4 News, 10 May 1984.

8. For much of this section I am indebted to R. J. Waller, *The Dukeries Transformed*, Oxford University Press, Oxford, 1983. See especially Chapter 4 on company villages and Chapter 5 on trade-unionism.

9. Nottinghamshire Working Miners' Committee internal documents.

10. C. Butcher, interview with the author.

11. *Daily Mirror*, 18 October 1984.

12. B. Copping, interview with the author.

13. *The Times*, 13 September 1984.

14. ITN Channel 4 News, 28 September 1984.

CHAPTER 9: A Question of Leadership

1. A. Scargill, *Marxism Today*, April 1981.

2. Quoted in R. Harris, *The Making of Neil Kinnock*, p. 164, Faber and Faber, London, 1984.

3. V. L. Allen, *The Militancy of British Miners*, p. 140. Moor Press, Shipley, 1981.

4. Quoted in the *Guardian*, 21 October 1982.

5. Quoted in the *Illustrated London News*, July 1978.

6. P. Noble, quoted in *The Times*, 8 January 1983.

7. F. Locke, quoted in the *Daily Telegraph* and *The Times*, 11 January 1983.

8. Quoted in the *Daily Telegraph*, 26 June 1980.

9. I. MacGregor, interview with the author for ITN Channel 4 News, untransmitted section.

10. See his interview with J. Reid in the *Glasgow Herald*, 5 October 1982, reproduced in J. Reid, *As I Please*, Mainstream, Edinburgh, 1984.

11. P. Tait, interview with the author.

12. Quoted in *The Times*, 13 May 1981.

13. J. Mortimer, *In Character*, p. 62, Penguin, Harmondsworth, 1984.

14. BBC 2 *Futures*, 30 September 1982.

15. *Daily Mirror*, 25 November 1980.

16. *Futures* (see note 13).

17. Quoted in the *Sun*, 9 September 1975.

18. Quoted in the *Illustrated London News*, July 1978.

19. Letter from A. Scargill to J. Cunningham, quoted in the *Guardian*, 9 September 1983.

20. A. Scargill, 'The New Unionism', *New Left Review*, 92, July/August 1975, p. 33.

21. *Marxism Today* (see note 1).

22. *Morning Star*, 2 July 1983.

23. *New Left Review* (see note 18), p. 27.

24. *Marxism Today* (see note 1).
25. Quoted in *Personnel Management*, April 1982.
26. Quoted in the *Sunday Times*, 28 October 1984.
27. *Marxism Today* (see note 1).
28. J. Reid, the *Spectator*, 13 October 1984.
29. *New Left Review* (see note 18), p. 31.
30. A. Scargill, interview with TV-am, 18 September 1983.
31. *Futures* (see note 13).
32. Ibid.
33. Account of BBC 2 *Newsday* interview, the *Listener*, 23 October 1975.
34. Account of BBC 1 *Person to Person* interview, the *Listener*, 9 August 1979.

CONCLUSION

1. Interview for Radio Hallam series *Down to Earth*, 1979.

Selective Bibliography

ALLEN, V. L., *The Militancy of British Miners*, Moor Press, Shipley, 1981.

CLUTTERBUCK, R., *Britain in Agony: The Growth of Industrial Violence*, Faber and Faber, London, 1978.

DROMEY, J., and TAYLOR, G., *Grunwick: The Workers' Story*, Lawrence and Wishart, London, 1978.

FERRIS, P., *The New Militants: Crisis in the Trade Unions*, Penguin, Harmondsworth, 1972.

GORMLEY, J., *Battered Cherub*, Hamish Hamilton, London, 1982.

GRIFFIN, A., *Mining in the East Midlands, 1550–1947*, Cass, London, 1971.

GRIFFIN, A., *The Miners of Nottinghamshire: 1914–1944*, Allen and Unwin, London, 1962.

HALL, T., *King Coal: Miners, Coal and Britain's Industrial Future*, Penguin, Harmondsworth, 1981.

HORNER, A., *Incorrigible Rebel*, MacGibbon and Kee, London, 1960.

HUGHES, J., and MOORE, R. (eds.), *A Special Case? Social Justice and the Miners*, Penguin, Harmondsworth, 1972.

MCCORMICK, B., *Industrial Relations in the British Coal Industry*, Macmillan, London, 1978.

MORTIMER, J., *In Character*, Penguin, Harmondsworth, 1984.

PAGE-ARNOT, R., *The Miners in Crisis and War*, Allen and Unwin, London, 1961.

PAGE-ARNOT, R., *The Miners: One Union, One Industry*, Allen and Unwin, London, 1979.

PAYNTER, W., *My Generation*, Allen and Unwin, London, 1972.

PITT, M., *The World on our Backs*, Lawrence and Wishart, London, 1979.

ROBENS, Lord, *Ten Year Stint*, Cassell, London, 1972.

SCARGILL, A., 'The New Unionism' (interview), *New Left Review*, 92, July/August 1975.

TAYLOR, A., *The Politics of the Yorkshire Miners*, Croom Helm, London, 1984.

TAYLOR, R., *The Fifth Estate: Britain's Unions in the Modern World* (revised edition), Pan, London, 1980.

TAYLOR, Lord, *Up Hill All The Way: A Miner's Struggle*, Sidgwick and Jackson, London, 1972.

WALLER, R. J., *The Dukeries Transformed: The Social and Political Development of a Twentieth-Century Coalfield*, Oxford University Press, Oxford, 1983.

WILSON, H., *Final Term: The Labour Government 1974–1976*, Weidenfeld and Nicolson, London, 1979.